THE FILMS
OF
HAROLD PINTER

THE **SUNY** SERIES

CULTURAL STUDIES IN CINEMA/VIDEO

WHEELER WINSTON DIXON | EDITOR

THE FILMS
OF
HAROLD PINTER

Edited by

STEVEN H. GALE

STATE UNIVERSITY OF NEW YORK PRESS

Published by
State University of New York Press, Albany

For information, address State University of New York Press,
90 State Street, Suite 700, Albany, NY 12207

Production by Marilyn P. Semerad
Marketing by Michael Campochiaro

Library of Congress Cataloging-in-Publication Data

The films of Harold Pinter / edited by Steven H. Gale.
    p. cm. — (SUNY series, cultural studies in cinema/video)
Includes index.
ISBN 0-7914-4931-9 (alk. paper) — ISBN 0-7914-4932-7 (pbk. : alk. paper)
    1. Pinter, Harold, 1930—Motion picture plays. 2. Pinter, Harold, 1930—Film and
video adaptations. 3. Motion pictures and literature. I. Gale, Steven H. II. Series.

PR6066.I53 Z6454 2001
791.43'75—dc21
                                                                            00-046415

10 9 8 7 6 5 4 3 2 1

CONTENTS

⌗

ILLUSTRATIONS

⊞

ACKNOWLEDGMENTS

—————————————— ⊞ ——————————————

The Films of Harold Pinter could not have been published if I had not had a great deal of support. Pinter's openness and willingness to talk with me and to answer questions that I have posed in numerous letters over the years were invaluable. I have always found him generous in providing me with material in the form of unpublished scripts and other materials, and I thank him for this. The contributors to this volume were especially helpful; they were interested in the project, timely in their submissions, and open to editorial suggestions. In addition, I appreciate the help provided by the State University of New York Press, and in particular the advice of Wheeler Winston Dixon, series editor, and acquisitions editors, Clay Morgan and James Peltz. Thanks also to production editor, Marilyn Semerad.

Along the way I also had help in obtaining materials from Lori Muha at Kentucky State University's Blazer Library and the reference librarians at the State Libraries and Archives and at the Paul Sawyer Library in Frankfort, Kentucky (Beverly Kunkle, Mildred Polsgrove, Rita Douthitt, Glen Lewis, Nancy Rice, and Mary Greathouse). Their time-consuming efforts and often necessarily quite inventive approaches to collecting material for me went well beyond the call of duty.

Among the scholars who freely gave of their time and resources were Chris Hudgins , Francis Gillen, Katherine Burkman, Tom Adler, and others. My secretary, Kim Bickers, aided me by checking sources, helping with the correspondence, typing, and all of the other details that go into producing a manuscript.

As always, my father and Linda provided moral support, and, as always, I want to thank my wife, Kathy, and my three daughters, Shannon, Ashley, and Heather, for their motivation, inspiration, and help, and especially for their patience and love.

INTRODUCTION

⊞

While Harold Pinter is considered one of the premier dramatists of the twentieth century, for years he also has been a master screenwriter. Unfortunately, relatively little critical attention has been paid to this large segment of his canon. Over a period of four decades, Pinter has written twenty-four film scripts, yet there has been only one book-length scholarly study of this part of his canon (published in 1985, it contains only analyses of his adaptations of other writers' work, the scripts are examined from a narrow literary point of view, and scant attention is paid to the cinematic elements).

In the 1980s and 1990s, Pinter's artistic attention has been focused almost exclusively on his screenwriting. Since his first scripted film, *The Servant*, appeared in 1962, he has had numerous cinematic successes, in terms of both popular acceptance and critical acclaim, and he has won several prestigious awards for his work. Besides being entered in major festivals, Pinter's films have been listed among the year's ten best consistently, and he received the Berlin Film Festival Silver Bear and an Edinburgh Festival Certificate of Merit for *The Caretaker*; the British Screenwriters Guild Award and the New York Film Critics' Best Writing Award for *The Servant*; the British Film Academy Award for *The Pumpkin Eater*; the Cannes Film Festival Special Jury Prize and a National Board of Review Award for *Accident*; the Cannes Film Festival Golden Palm for Best Film and the British Academy Award for *The Go-Between*, and a National Board of Review Best English-Language Film Award for *The Last Tycoon*. His more recent films, *The French Lieutenant's Woman*, *Betrayal*, *Turtle Diary*, *The Handmaid's Tale*, and *The Trial* have received equal praise. Indeed, critics claim that Pinter's distinctive style and unmis-

1

takable writing ability have been responsible for the best work done by several of his directors (as I documented in *Butter's Going Up*).

The breadth of Pinter's screenwriting talent is demonstrated in the range of his sources. Of his filmscripts, four are adaptations of his own dramas: *Betrayal, The Birthday Party, The Caretaker,* and *The Homecoming.* At least fourteen of his other plays, *The Basement, The Collection, The Dumb Waiter, The Lover, No Man's Land, The Hothouse, Mountain Language, Night School, A Night Out, One for the Road, Old Times, Party Time, The Room,* and *Tea Party,* as well as *Pinter People* (a cartoon compilation of some of his revue sketches), have been produced on television, some of them more than once. Pinter has adapted two films from another dramatist's play, Simon Gray's *Butley* and William Shakespeare's *King Lear.* Sixteen of the remaining seventeen filmscripts are cinematic translations of other writers' novels: Nicholas Mosley's *Accident,* Adam Hall's *The Berlin Memorandum* (released as *The Quiller Memorandum*), Ian McEwan's *The Comfort of Strangers,* John Fowles's *The French Lieutenant's Woman,* L. P. Hartley's *The Go-Between,* Margaret Atwood's *The Handmaid's Tale,* Aidan Higgins' *Langrishe, Go Down,* F. Scott Fitzgerald's *The Last Tycoon,* Vladimir Nabokov's *Lolita* (published but not filmed), Penelope Mortimer's *The Pumpkin Eater,* Marcel Proust's *A la recherche du temps perdu* (*Remembrance of Things Past,* published but never filmed), Kazuo Ishiguro's *The Remains of the Day* (Pinter took his name off the project), Fred Uhlmann's *Reunion,* Robin Maugham's *The Servant,* Franz Kafka's *The Trial,* Russell Hoban's *The Turtle Diary,* and Joseph Conrad's *Victory* (published but not yet filmed). Furthermore, he worked on a screenplay version of *The Diaries of Etty Hillesum,* a Holocaust narrative, in 1996, although the project did not go forward, and he completed an adaptation of Isak Dinesen's short story "The Dreaming Child" in 1997. The screenwriter has also written several television adaptations, including a filmed version of Elizabeth Bowen's *The Heat of the Day,* and it is important to note that in answer to questions about the difference between his work in television and film, he said that he makes "no distinction between working for television and feature film."[1]

Because of the nature of filmmaking (which frequently ends up with a product that only partially resembles the original screenplay[2]), the authors of the ten chapters contained in *The Films of Harold Pinter* focus more on the screenplays than on the films made from those scripts, though discussion of the movie itself is included in many of the chapters. The pieces are presented in the chronological order in which the movies were released (or the date of composition in those cases in which no films has been made). They will provide information for students and scholars who are interested in Pinter, film (including the art of adaptation), drama, the novel, British and American literature, the specific films, and the specific source novels. In addition, because the finished scripts are compared to Pinter's sources, most of these chapters also include insights into both the differences between the media and the screenwriter's creative processes.

In his chapter "'Swift Strokes': *The Pumpkin Eater*—The Adaptive Screenplay as a Unique Text" William L. Horne examines Pinter's adaptation of Mortimer's novel. In "The Eternal Summer of Joseph Losey and Harold Pinter's *Accident*," Wheeler Winston Dixon considers how the concepts of eternal youth and endless summers are linked in *Accident* and comments on photographer Gerry Fisher's use of light to reinforce these themes. "The Ecology of *The Go-Between*" is Marya Bednerik's discussion of Pinter's use of natural settings as both images and symbols to explore the interrelationships of organisms, species, and communities of species in *The Go-Between*—the relationships between culture and landscapes, time and space, and so on. "The Tragedy of Illusion: Harold Pinter and *The Last Tycoon*," by Katherine H. Burkman and Mijeong Kim, is a demonstration of how Pinter, using a cinematic metaphor from the novel, both successfully adapted Fitzgerald's *The Last Tycoon* for the screen and at the same time created a work of art in its own right. In "*The French Lieutenant's Woman*: Harold Pinter's Masterpiece of Cinematic Adaptation," Steven H. Gale examines Pinter's use of cinematic techniques to adapt Fowles's *The French Lieutenant's Woman* and at the same time create a film masterpiece that surpasses its source. In "Daddy Dearest: Harold Pinter's *The Comfort of Strangers*," Ann S. Hall discusses the concept of patriarchy as a cultural element that underlies the action in the screenwriter's adaptation. Edward T. Jones's "On *The Remains of the Day*: Pinter Remaindered" is a comparison of Pinter's and Ruth Prawer Jhabvala's adaptations of *The Remains of the Day*, with reference to the source novel by Ishiguro. Louis Marks's informative and enlightening recollections of how Pinter's adaptation of Kafka came to be filmed are contained in his fascinating "Producing *The Trial*: A Personal Memoir." Christopher C. Hudgins provides an analysis of Pinter's script for Nabokov's *Lolita* and its development in "Harold Pinter's *Lolita*: 'My Sin, My Soul.'" Finally, Pinter's latest screenplay, an unfilmed adaptation of a Dinesen tale is the subject of Francis X. Gillen's "Isak Dinesen with a Contemporary Social

Conscience: Harold Pinter's Film Adaptation of 'The Dreaming Child,'" in which Gillen shows how Pinter creates new characters and adds dialogue to introduce a modern perspective into the Victorian story.

NOTES

1. Harold Pinter, "Writing for myself," *Twentieth Century*, 169 (February 1961): 172–75.

2. As Jeff Arch, author of *Sleepless in Seattle*, says, "When you cash the check, the screenplay is no longer yours" (conversation with Steven Gale, Maui Writers Conference, 1998). In other words, once they have purchased it, it is their property and the production company and director can do anything with the script that they want to. Several of the essays document Pinter's experience with this problem.

FIGURE 1. *The Pumpkin Eater*. Anne Bancroft as Jo and Peter Finch as her husband, Jake Armitage. Royal Films International. Jerry Ohlinger Archives.

CHAPTER ONE

⊞

"Swift Strokes": The Pumpkin Eater— The Adaptive Screenplay as a Unique Text

WILLIAM L. HORNE

PHILPOT: . . . but of course his understanding is so extraordinary, his innate . . . the way he draws his characters . . . swift strokes . . . so swift . . .

—Harold Pinter, *The Pumpkin Eater*

In common with most adaptive screenplays, Harold Pinter's *The Pumpkin Eater* has been squeezed into near asphyxiation by works with more established claims to authentic aesthetic identity: on the one hand, the novel and, on the other, the film. Pinter may have been awarded the British Film Academy Award for the best screenplay of 1964 for this work, but exactly what was being honored is questionable. Clearly, the screenplay in this context represents not a prior text for performance but rather is an amorphous conception of the writer's contribution to the spoken language and to the narrative structure of the film. For some, the script is simply confused with the dialogue: Brendan Gill writes in the *New Yorker* of "the benefit of a dazzling screenplay by that master of oral shorthand."[1] For others, the screenplay disappears behind the novel: John Coleman argues in the *New Statesman* that "you don't bring such an anyway idiosyncratic talent in to do work that has already been done."[2] Such a comment indicates a total failure to appreciate the integrity of Pinter's screenplay *The Pumpkin Eater* as a work separate and different from novel and film. Its structure is the result of an active process of engagement with the source. Intentional choices are reflected in a screenplay which is a complete and independent text.

Among the prolific academic critics of Pinter's efforts, even those few who acknowledge the value of his work with Joseph Losey, most summarily dismiss the other screenplays. In an usually cogent monologue, John Russell Taylor describes *The Pumpkin Eater* as a mere "essay in writing technique."[3] Arnold Hinchliffe barely masks his disdain in labeling it "an unusual choice."[4] Yet, this script is central to an understanding of Pinter's development as a writer for the screen. One can clearly distinguish the seeds of those characteristic preoccupations which grow to blossom in *Accident* (1967) and come to mature fruition in *The Go-Between* (1969). Thus, *The Pumpkin Eater* represents a crucial stage in the screenwriter's engagement with the formal problems of writing for the cinema, particularly in his ongoing efforts to find appropriate means to express the effects of time upon the workings of a single consciousness.

Penelope Mortimer is not a major novelist. In keeping with a great deal of contemporary fiction, she writes of attendant lords rather than of Hamlet. Nevertheless, though her range is circumscribed, her achievement within it is considerable; she has been aptly described as "a poet of our small boredoms and unhappinesses."[5] *The Pumpkin Eater* is usually well and sensitively written, and even occasionally brilliant. However, ever since Virginia Woolf's *Mrs. Dalloway,* the great danger of stream-of-consciousness novels has been a certain self-indulgence, which tends to encourage the writer to produce ornate and highly stylized passages at the expense of clarity and order. Despite an occasional tendency to lapse into such impressionistic follies, as in the predictable dream sequence in which Jake drowns clutching a blade of grass, Mortimer largely avoids such pitfalls.[6] The self-portrait of Jo Armitage is carefully constructed in a series of well-observed sequences. The process is described in the preface:

It is the piecing together of a human being in a number of apparently unrelated scenes, many presented out of time sequence but with a steady logic of their own, and so beautifully selected, so carefully juxtaposed, that a pattern soon emerges. (3)

In the opening pages of the novel we are presented with a *fait accompli*: the heroine has already suffered her nervous breakdown. The chapters that follow articulate the progress of her marriage to Jake while examining the causes and the effects of her collapse. Midway through the book we return to the period dealt with in the first chapter; indeed, we see her once more on the couch of Freudian analysis.

The novel is based upon the notion of a confession; the narrator seeks to express her feelings and explain her actions to the reader:

"Well," I said, "I will try. I honestly will try to be honest with you, although I suppose really what you're more interested in is my not being honest, if you see what I mean." (9)

Her statement of purpose to her doctor, the opening paragraph of the work, is all the more significant because its sentiments are repeated in the short epilogue to the final chapter:

I have tried to be honest with you, although I suppose that you would really have been more interested in my not being honest. Some of these things happened, and some were dreams. They are all true, as I understand truth. They are all real, as I understand reality. (222)

There is something particularly annoying in this pronouncement of the insubstantial quality of subjective reality. It smacks rather of the young child, afraid of the power of his or her own imagination, who ends a fanciful story with "and then I woke up." Here, Mortimer falls victim to the same self-conscious trickiness that causes her to avoid ever naming her heroine or numbering her brood.

The very fact that Pinter chose to adapt Mortimer's novel for the screen has confounded many of his critics. Martin Esslin finds the book "remote from Pinter's own preoccupations,"[7] and Hinchliffe argues that "Pinter and the novel were inappropriate companions."[8] Their misgivings are the product of a blinkered and chauvinistic view of the book. For them, as for many of the reviewers, it is "very much a 'woman's novel,'"[9] and this label is applied in a highly pejorative tone. Because Jack Clayton has directed a film that writers in the popular press characterize as "a woman's picture all right,"[10] the screenplay is duly tarred with the same brush. William Baker and Stephen Tabachnick are typical in claiming that "Pinter accepted a challenge to his emotional insightfulness and flexibility. By the very nature of its subject—the need to make babies—*The Pumpkin Eater* demands a special feminine empathy."[11] There is little doubt that such critical misgivings about Pinter's choice of material spring from a feeling that he failed to demonstrate "a special feminine empathy" in his early works for the stage. After all, women do play subordinate roles. Meg, in *The Birthday Party* (1958), like her spiritual sister, Rose, in *The Room*, is a slight figure who functions in a much narrower range than Goldberg or Stanley. In *The Dumb Waiter, The Caretaker*, and *The Dwarfs*, Pinter deals exclusively with males. Still, he has strenuously denied any deliberate bias against female characters. In 1966, he even claimed that he would "like to write a play . . . entirely about women."[12] But even Ruth, who plays a substantial part in the unfolding of *The Homecoming* (1965), often seems to be more a product of male fantasies, a combination mother and whore, than a fully sentient individual; she certainly lacks the vitality of a Max or a Lenny.

While it is true that such a concentrated examination of a female character is uncharacteristic of Pinter's early work for the theatre, it is a critical blind alley to approach the screenplay of *The Pumpkin Eater* by way of his "feminine empathy" or the lack of it. Baker and Tabachnick, like many other critics, base their arguments on a distorted view of the novel and, hence, of Pinter's adaptation. Neither work is a mere treatise on the "need to make babies." As Mortimer explained to a reporter from the *Daily Telegraph*: "*The Pumpkin Eater* is about the progression of the married state."[13] But, more importantly, it examines the effects of an intimate relationship upon the mind of a sensitive individual. Pinter answered an interviewer's question about his reasons for writing this script with his customary irony: "Because it's about marriage. And marriage is important. I mean a lot of people do it."[14] Nevertheless, his attraction to the novel goes much deeper. As with *Accident* and *The Go-Between*, he is drawn to this attempt to examine the workings of a single mind in crisis. Pinter chose to adapt this work because it presented him with a formal problem that has continued to engage his interest in the cinema: the attempt to express a subjective perspective.

An examination of the screenplay as a consequence of the adapter's response to the novel allows us to estimate the significance of intentional meanings. The process of purposeful choice, modification, and restructuring in the new form is partly the product of the adapter's selective interpretation of the source, but it is also the result of his perception of the unique aesthetic requirements of the screenplay as a text for performance on screen. So, the nature of his response to the novel is conditioned by the form in which he works. Mortimer's work provides Pinter with a clear indication of the kind of structure that he should use in the creation of the screenplay.

The novel begins in the midst of one of the narrator's sessions with her psychiatrist; the scene allows Mortimer both to suggest the profound angst of her heroine and to establish some of the basic facts of her life. On occasion, these details seem a little too deliberately contrived to set the scene: "It's very simple. Jake is rich. He makes about £50,000 a year. I suppose you'd call that rich. But everything is covered with dust" (10). This first chapter ends as the session draws to a close with the psychiatrist's pompous unction: "'We shall, I think, make progress,' he said" (16). With startling impact, the second chapter begins in the middle of a scene thirteen years earlier: marriage is discussed with the skeptical father of the groom: "Jake's father said, 'I suppose you know what you're doing. What do the children say?'" (17).

This instant plunge into the waters of the past clearly suggests to Pinter his modus operandi, yet he has chosen to make substantial adjustments in the nature of this structure. He avoids opening on Jo's meeting with her psychiatrist. Such a base for a series of flashbacks would have produced some rather tired and counterproductive clichés of the cinema. Pinter integrates his flashbacks into the morning on which Jo suffers her traumatic crying spell in Harrods. Such a structural adjustment is very much in keeping with Pinter's overall attempt to tighten the construct and to place the emphasis firmly upon the impending personal crisis.

The most significant changes that he makes involve his attempts to convert the more subdued elements of the novel into clear-cut dramatic situations. In seeking to articulate the mental dislocation of his heroine, he must embody her dilemma. Where the novelist is able to examine her thoughts and perceptions explicitly, the screenwriter must focus stringently upon her reactions to experience. So, he structures his work in order to place the maximum emphasis upon moments of crisis. Typical of this method is the way in which he interprets and recasts Jake's discovery that Jo is pregnant again. In the novel, the narrator writes to her husband to give him the news:

> I told him that my father was dead and that to take her mind off it I had told my mother that I was pregnant. I said it had taken her mind off it wonderfully, so far; and that it also happened to be true. (131)

In the following chapter, Jake arrives for the cremation, pale, haggard, and bursting with righteous indignation. Pinter nicely abandons the arbitrary device of the letter and produces something of a cinematic coup de grace: as they walk in the garden, Jo's mother upbraids Jake for a crime that he does not yet know that he has committed:

> MOTHER: Oh, I don't know what George would have said if he knew.
>
> JAKE: Mmmm? About what?
>
> JO: You could let this off for allotments, couldn't you?[15]

The irony is carefully calculated to contribute to the building of tension:

> *Jake looks at Jo*
>
> JAKE: Live to see what?
>
> *Pause*
>
> MOTHER: On top of everything else. As if she hasn't got enough. Mind you, he always loved them, he loved the children.
>
> *Jake stands still and stares at Jo.* (*F.S.*, 106)

Here is a very clear example of the nature of the adaptive process. The recasting of an incident in the novel begins as a purely formal matter. The weak device of the letter is replaced by a scene that develops toward the critical moment of revelation. But, in the process, meaning is significantly changed. It is true that Mortimer is able to articulate the innermost thoughts of her narrator: "I have been apprehensive, now I was frightened. I prayed, but not for my burning father. Let it all be all right. Make it all right. Stop him looking at me like that" (*P.E.*, 135–36).

However, in the screenplay Jo's suffering is all the more powerful because it is implied rather than explicitly stated. Pinter makes consummate use, with all of its consequent irony, of the cinema's ability to provide its spectators with knowledge denied to some of its participants. Moreover, he effectively articulates Jo's horror and fear by employing the capacity of the medium to present simultaneously a seemingly objective view of the situation and her perspective on it.

There is an abundance of indications throughout the screenplay that Pinter intended his work to be interpreted in film as an intense study of a mind in breakdown. As a reviewer suggested in the *Times Literary Supplement,* "The dialogue, all the dialogue, not just the odd isolated scene—comes over as curiously feverish, nightmarishly heightened, and we get very clearly the idea that we are seeing through the neurotic Jo's eyes and hearing through her ears."[16] But the attempt to employ Jo's subjective perception goes far beyond the dialogue into the very structure of the work and its suggested cinematic interpretation.

In his notational instructions, Pinter clearly indicates that he wishes members of the audience to be aware that they are seeing through Jo's eyes. At the end of the first flashback to her initial meeting with Jake, he includes a crucial series of production directions:

> *Close-up. Jake looking at her.*
>
> *Close-up. Jo.*
>
> *Back to Giles holding up three planks of partition, examining them. One plank falls.*
>
> *Plank falling.*
>
> *Large close-up.*
>
> *Jake kissing Jo's ear.*
>
> *(No background noise). (F.S., 67)*

A carefully developed series of suggested images encompass the potential shift in Jo's relationship from her past to her future husband; the images are given their significance by Jo's role as a functioning editor, the source of a distinct point of view. The potential intimacy suggested by the close-ups of Jake and Jo, given connected meaning by *her* self-consciousness, is contrasted with a sense of alienation from her current husband, implied in the medium shot of Giles. At this point, Pinter makes full use of the notion that what we see is the product of Jo's perspective: "*One plank falls. Plank falling.*"

From the image as realistic photographic representation of a particular incident, there is an immediate transition to the image as symbolic index of the disintegration of the relationship between Giles and Jo. Clearly, it is suggested that Jo selects and orders the sequence and abstracts an image from its context in order to emphasize its significance. This notion is further developed in the "*Large close-up,*" which follows "*JAKE kissing Jo's ear.*" This suggestive image is rendered all the more tellingly a product of Jo's consciousness by the surreal absence of background noise. In order to communicate the idea that the mind recreates past experience in an ordered manner, which imposes significance on that which is selectively represented, Pinter indicates a momentary divorcement of the soundtrack from the image. This is a technique that he continues to refine and develop in his subsequent screenplays *Accident* and *The Go-Between*. He is fully exploring the unique formal possibilities of the cinema.

What makes this sequence all the more interesting, though, is that it reveals itself fully as the consequence of Pinter's response to the source novel. Of course, the whole notion of the expression of Jo's subjective perspective in film is the result of his engagement with Mortimer's first-person narrative. But, in more specific terms, his reading of the novel leads him to extract a suggestion to be modified and employed as the central focus for this sequence of images. The narrator tells her psychiatrist that Giles had constructed a series of hardboard partitions to divide up the barn in which they lived: "After a bit they got very shaky and some of them fell down, but by that time I think Giles knew that it was all over so he didn't bother to fix them up again" (*P.E.*, 104). Here is a palpable indication of the nature of the adapter's active engagement with his source material. The process of reading, of necessity, involves interpretation; the reader creates the meaning of the text for himself. Selective emphases lead to significant choices of what to extract and what to modify for employment in the new formal construct.

The single most interesting use of cinematic devices in the screenplay is in the cocktail party scene, given by Jo for the assembled film crew on their return from Morocco. It represents the most successful aspect of Pinter's attempt to make use of film's simultaneous ability to render an apparently objective portrait of a situation together with its capacity to endorse a single point of view. Jo's perspective is fully integrated with Pinter's continuing examination of the English social fabric. In discussing his work as the director of *Butley* (1974), Pinter referred to the advantages of the stringent control afforded by the cinema. On the stage, a major challenge is "how to insist that the focus of the audience goes in one specific direction when there are so many other things to look at on the stage. With a film the audience must attend only to the particular image you're showing them."[17]

In the cocktail party sequence he exploits the capacity of the medium to manipulate the attention of the audience with speed and precision. He employs a more sophisticated version of a technique that he employed effectively in *The Servant* (1963). Losey praised Pinter for his appreciation of "the usefulness of the overheard line: of dialogue used as sound effect,"[18] and the fragments of speech in the restaurant scene in *The Servant* help both to create the necessary mood and to act as an oblique and wickedly amusing choral commentary on the situation of the major characters. But, for the party scene in *The Pumpkin Eater*, this device becomes the veritable foundation of its structure: multiple strands of conversation are delicately interlaced in the creation of the complex fabric of Jo's perspective.

The reviewer for the *Times Literary Supplement* proved delighted by "how brilliantly, and odiously, Mrs. Mortimer described the good-time vulgarity of Jake's film world!"[19] Her narrator is ever ready with an acute observation or an ironic aside: "The cameraman was curled up on the continuity girl's lap, nuzzling into her mohair breast" (*P.E.*, 119). Hurst is presented as a drunken buffoon who comes out with remarks like "Deathville, as far as I'm concerned" (*P.E.*, 118) and greets someone with "Darling! My Angel! (*P.E.*, 119). Yet the narrator feels able to tell Dinah: "I rather like him" (*P.E.*, 119). She manages to separate her amused contempt for these hopelessly shallow people from her visceral loathing of Conway. Pinter responds to both aspects of her perspective to create a tightly structured and highly effective scene. Nevertheless, his major stimulus undoubtedly comes from an intimate expression of the narrator's feelings: "I seemed to go from trap to trap. I finished the champagne hoping it would quell a rising despair" (*P.E.*, 120). The screenwriter nicely articulates her view of the party as a developing crescendo of despair.

Far removed from the diffuse quality of the novel, the scene is very carefully fashioned. It has all of that "necessary shape" of which Pinter spoke so eloquently in his speech accepting the Shakespeare Prize in Hamburg.[20] In his directions, at the beginning of the piece, it is clearly established that we are viewing the sequence from Jo's perspective:

Both rooms are crowded with people. Concentrated party noise. Jo's face. Conway is hemming her into a corner, talking. (*F.S.*, 97–98)

Having finally escaped from the clutches of the odious Conway, Jo proceeds to move through the groups of guests. Once again, Pinter makes it apparent that we are experiencing her perceptions: *"Jo moves away. Camera follows her as she moves. Snatches of conversation overheard"* (*F.S.*, 98).

The hearty rendition of the unlikely story about the would-be sadist is carefully intertwined with fragments of other dialogue:

GUEST TWO: But it's got nothing to do with you, darling.

GUEST ONE: He was a very nice chap, you see, very quiet sort of bloke . . .

GUEST THREE: It has absolutely everything to do with me as a matter of fact. (*F.S.*, 98)

The comic vitality of the sequence is not simply an end in itself. The oblique references to Jo's situation are apparent: a thin layer of good manners barely conceals the hostility between Guest Two and Guest Three, and the central story concerns a man who "wanted more than anything else . . . to beat up a woman" (*F.S.*, 98). The sequence builds to an indictment of the moral turpitude of these unthinking members of the bourgeoisie. Having heard someone speak of potential financial rewards, "at least fifteen grand," we are presented with the filmmakers' view of Morocco and its inhabitants:

GUEST SIX: I had three showers a day—absolutely every single day.

GUEST SEVEN: What were the peasants like?

GUEST EIGHT: Extraordinarily interesting. Fascinating faces.

GUEST SEVEN: Lots of character, I suppose.

GUEST EIGHT: Oh lots, lots. (*F.S.*, 99)

In their patronizing condescension, these characters are kindred spirits of the effete Mountsets in *The Servant* and the supercilious Denys in *The Go-Between*. Pinter is delicately manipulating the documentary naturalism of film form to realize effective political parody.

The midpoint of the scene is carefully contrived to establish a parallel with its beginning. We have seen Jo trapped by Conway; now a short exchange with her daughter provides a view of their respective spouses:

DINAH: Marvellous. Dad's really with it tonight, isn't he? I didn't know Beth Conway had red hair. I thought it was sort of blonde. She's lovely isn't she? (*F.S.* 99)

Pinter specifies that he expects the director to cut to an image of Jake, all too willingly trapped by Beth:

Beth. Dinah's point of view, lying on couch, talking to Jake and surrounded by people. Back to scene. (*F.S.*, 99)

The stage direction "*Back to scene*" is highly significant, for it suggests that the writer intends this shot to disrupt the pattern of Jo's progression around the room, in order to heighten and to justify her sense of impending disaster. The screenwriter is deliberately emphasizing the duality of the medium, its ability to present a view that encompasses that of Jo.

Pinter indicates the return to a fluid, subjective style by repeating his earlier direction: "*She moves away, camera with her. Snatches of conversation*" (*F.S., 99*). As we follow her, the fragments become shorter and more frenzied:

GUEST ONE: . . . at last, at last, they stood there stark naked, looking at each other. He had the cane in his hand . . .

GUEST NINE: It'll be a smash, and believe me, when I say smash . . . (*F.S.*, 99)

The writer utilizes seemingly unrelated pieces of dialogue to comically punctuate and comment upon the downfall of the unfortunate misogynist, who raises rather more cane than he anticipates:

GUEST ONE: He saw that she was holding a cane too. "What's all this?" he said.

GUEST THIRTEEN: Actually, you really are terribly masculine.

GUEST FOURTEEN: Am I really?

GUEST ONE: Suddenly she whacked him with all her might. "Oww!" he screamed. (*F.S.*, 100)

The cozy affectation of the "terribly masculine" beau and his syco-phant counterpoints the punch line of the story. For Jo, the situation retains all of the claustrophobic intensity of nightmare. Her insecurities as a victimized woman are distorted into a bizarre shadow play, whose comic form accentuates its horror. Fittingly, it leads up to the point at which she joins Beth, Jake, and Conway around the couch. The struc-ture of the scene is formally complete. Her initial sortie is sandwiched between the obsequious Conway and a disquieting view of Jake and Beth. The second progress ends in a coming together of the disastrous *ménage à quatre.*

Throughout the screenplay, both the dialogue that is selected and extracted from the novel to be reshaped and that which is wholly invented contain clear indications of Pinter's continuing concerns, which are very different from Mortimer's. Inevitably, a major element in this examina-tion of a woman dislocated from her social role is her felt difficulty in establishing the realities of her existence. Like so many of Pinter's charac-ters, she uses language in an attempt to locate fixed boundaries which can define the limits of her experience. One of Pinter's continued preoccupa-tions has been the intense difficulty of achieving such a personal certainty. His characters desperately want to achieve absolute knowledge about themselves and their environment, but they are ever struggling in the shifting sands, unable to find a fixed point in a relentlessly mobile uni-verse. In 1962, at a student drama festival, Pinter spoke of the impossi-bility of verifying past experience: "I don't mean merely years ago, but yes-terday, this morning. What took place, what was the nature of what took place, what happened?"[21]

Jo desperately tries to goad Jake into providing her with specific details of his relationship with the devious Philpot:

JAKE: It was nothing, nothing. Don't you understand?

JO: What do you mean, nothing?

Pause.

What do you mean, nothing?

JAKE: What do you think I mean? (*F.S.*, 78)

The confrontation proceeds by repetitive fits and starts. Jo's desire to know exactly what happened is met with a smokescreen of evasion:

JO: What did you catch her for?

JAKE: I didn't catch her!

JO: She fainted.

JAKE: What does it matter if I caught her or not? I didn't catch her. It doesn't matter, can't you understand? Who cares? (*F.S.*, 78–79)

As Jo seeks certainty about what has occurred in the past, Jake fights one of those "desperate rearguard attempts to keep ourselves to ourselves," which abound in Pinter's works.[22]

It is typical of this writer's technique that his character does not issue a simple denial—he qualifies it with attempts to disarm his accuser. These desperate ploys merely add to the suspicion that the truth is not being told. Bill, in *The Collection* (1963), is equally maddening in his denial of involvement with James's wife:

I was nowhere near Leeds last week, old chap. Nowhere near your wife either, I'm quite sure of that. Apart from that, I . . . just don't do such things. Not in my book.

Pause.

I wouldn't dream of it.[23]

The character's overpersistent attempt to assert moral probity merely throws his initial statement further into doubt. Pinter's point, as in the scene between Jake and Jo, is that it is ultimately impossible to verify what has occurred in the past. Moreover, what he once called "the highly ambiguous commerce"[24] of language simply adds to the confusion.

In *The Collection* we never discover whether Stella has been unfaithful or not. The play ends with James yet again trying to oblige her to make that definitive statement, which she continues to resist:

That's what you did.

Pause.

Didn't you.

> *Pause.*
>
> That's the truth . . . isn't it?
>
> *Stella looks at him, neither confirming nor denying.*[25]

As with William Shakespeare's *Othello*, it is not jealousy but doubt that becomes the "green-eyed monster." The beast may be satisfied only by a categorical confirmation of the worst. In the screenplay of *The Pumpkin Eater*, Jake's infidelity is never seriously in question, but Pinter is exploring the same territory: the desire to tame experience by defining it. And it is a territory that is wholly his own, removed from that of the novel. After Conway's revelation of Jake's indiscretions with Beth, Jo interrogates her husband less about this affair than about the more distant past: "Did you sleep with Philpot?" Jake's reluctant confessions are continually tempered with denials. Pinter is in his element, particularly in the carefully constructed ending of the scene:

> JAKE: What others?
>
> JO: How often?
>
> JAKE: There weren't any others.
>
> JO: Did you bring them here?
>
> JAKE: How could I bring them here?
>
> JO: Where did you take them?
>
> JAKE: It never happened. (*F.S.*, 122)

There is another clear parallel to *The Collection* in this work. The confrontation between Conway and Jake in the bar is strikingly similar to the battle between James and Bill:

> *James makes a sudden move forward.*
>
> *Bill starts back, and falls over a pouffe on to the floor. James chuckles. Pause.*
>
> BILL: You've made me spill my drink. You've made me spill it on my cardigan.[26]

Likewise, in the screenplay, the submerged anger breaks to the surface in an act of calculated violence:

Jake's glass slips from his hand, falls on Conway's lap and then to the floor. Whisky stains Conway's trousers.

CONWAY: You've made me wet. (*F.S.*, 131)

The nominal *raison d'être* for the scene comes from a passing reference by the narrator of the novel: "Jake told me that he had heard that Conway was roaming London blind drunk" (*P.E.*, 173). Yet, Pinter's bizarre, full-blown confrontation remains far removed in tone from the screenplay as a whole. It is the one scene in which Jo is not present. Its only justification might have been that it articulates the heroine's desire for revenge upon Conway. But, there is no evidence for this supposition in the scenes with Giles that precede and succeed it. One has to conclude that Pinter could not resist a perfect opportunity to indulge one of his dramatic preoccupations, the power struggle which frequently underlies conventional, polite conversation.

It is interesting that few if any English or American reviewers ever refer to this scene, yet various academic critics single it our for praise in their all too brief remarks about the film. For Esslin, it provides "passages of dialogue which bear his unmistakable hallmark" and justifies a liberal quotation.[27] Similarly, Baker and Tabachnick refer to "the dialogue of subtle conflict" and the "poison of Pinter's pen" in introducing their own illustration.[28] Even Daniel Salem feels that the scene is one of the best in the film because "l'humour sarcastique . . . fait merveille" ("sarcastic humor . . . works wonders").[29] All of these critics fall into the trap of extracting the sequence from the screenplay and judging it as an independent comic sketch. As such, it is a fine piece of idiosyncratic dramatic writing, but in context it seems somewhat inappropriate:

JAKE: How is your wife, by the way?

CONWAY: Tip top. She's at a reception tonight for the Duchess of Dubrovnik.

JAKE: I thought she *was* the Duchess of Dubrovnik.

CONWAY: My wife? No, no, not at all. Not at all. Not at all.

JAKE: (*laughing*): Well, you're not the bloody Duke anyway. (*F.S.*, 131)

The sequence borders upon the perilous quicksand of self-parody. It is a reminder that the adapter's reaction to elements in the source, coupled with a highly distinctive "signature," can lead to the inclusion of sequences that damage the overall coherence of the work.

A number of elements in the novel could have readily been created by Pinter. It is in the nature of the adaptive process that, in a sense, the screenwriter finds in the source what he wants to find. For instance, Mortimer's hopelessly naive young man, who comes to the door to advocate the banning of "the bomb," makes no appearance in the screenplay, despite the fact that a whole chapter of the novel is devoted to the narrator's reaction to him. Yet, the Jamaican "King of Israel," whose visit the narrator briefly describes to Giles, plays a prominent role. This is another significant indication of the nature of the adaptive process, for Pinter responds to this brief reference because the character is one that could well have appeared in one of his early plays. This strange figure provides him with the opportunity to engage in the bizarre and rather sinister comedy of which he is a master. Of course, Pinter angles the scene to emphasize the mesmeric nature of the man and the frightening quality of his intrusion. One can readily compare this menacing figure with the sudden entrance of the blind black man Riley in *The Room* and the foreboding presence of the mysterious, enigmatic match seller in *A Slight Ache* (1959). In an interview broadcast on the BBC European Service very early in his writing career, Pinter commented on the notion of the visitor disturbing the inhabitants of a confined space: "an intruder comes to upset the balance of everything, in other words points to the delusion on which she is basing her life."[30] Like the chorus in a Greek tragedy, the strange "King of Judah" proclaims that: "The people are unhappy because they give the gift of their love to unworthy men and unworthy women" (*P.E.*, 194). The screenplay follows this speech to the letter, but because it is afforded considerably more prominence than in the novel, it appears far more significant.

Like the subsequent cocktail party, the scene in the hairdressing salon is very much a part of Pinter's continuing examination of the English class system. The woman who addresses Jo and ultimately attacks her is far-removed from the indolent privileges of middle-class existence in St. John's Wood. As she tells Jo, in a detail culled directly from Meg Evans's letter in the novel, "I do a weekly wash in a copper boiler" (*F.S.*, 92). While the novel provides Pinter with the nominal stimulus for this scene, he radically alters the nature of this woman's role. In the book she appears solely in a letter which describes a life that is poor, nasty, brutish, and "*so hard to live*": "I clean ten rooms a week, two toilets, cook dinner every day for the six of us as well as keeping my little ones happy" (*P.E.*, 147–48).

The narrator is torn between conventional disdain and genuine sympathy. On the one hand, she snubs Mrs. Evans because she sends her message in "what I think they call a Manila envelope, such as they use for bills" (*P.E.*, 147). On the other hand, in mulling over various possible replies, she is ironic at the expense of her own privilege: "Dear Mrs. Evans, We all get what we deserve. I myself am not going to have another baby. Why not learn Italian or take up some useful . . ." (*P.E.*, 148). But above all, the letter is a convenient stimulus for a powerful aside in which the narrator comments on the overwhelming disadvantages of being born a woman: "Stop trying to be a man! Stop being such a bloody woman! You're too strong! You're too weak! Get out! Come back! (*P.E.*, 149). It enables Mortimer to provide a telling indictment of a society that defines women largely according to male expectations.

Certainly, this notion is also central to Pinter's conception, but far from being an excuse to vent an explicit grievance, the Woman in the Hairdresser's becomes a realized character. Pinter has responded to the rather overexplicit suggestion in the novel by creating a figure very much akin to the Cockneys who people his early plays. This woman has a good deal in common with Goldberg in *The Birthday Party* and Max in *The Homecoming*. The expansive *mensch* of the former and the capricious patriarch of the latter are, like her, rather comic, garrulous figures who manage to retain both pathos and a certain menace. Yet, the chinks in *her* armor are somewhat more apparent. She fails to display their seeming confidence: "I'm desirable. I'm not old. I know" (*F.S.*, 92). In her desperate attempt to sustain a private domain in which she can remain the only queen, she is closely aligned with the Meg of the closing sequence of *The Birthday Party*.

> MEG: I was the belle of the ball.
>
> PETEY: Were you?
>
> MEG: Oh yes. They all said I was.
>
> PETEY : I bet you were, too.
>
> MEG: Oh, it's true. I was.
>
> *Pause*
>
> I know I was.[31]

In the novel, Mrs. Evans's letter functions as an arbitrary *deus ex machina* to provide the narrator with the opportunity to indulge in a rather self-conscious aside: "Women aren't important" (*P.E.*, 148). Pinter responds to this by embedding the idea of female subjugation in the complex ironies of the anonymous woman's attack on Jo: "I think women are the only ones. . . . They're the only ones" (*F.S.*, 93). Throughout her discourse she has revealed that she defines herself purely in terms of traditional masculine stereotypes. Her attraction to her neighbor arises from the picture of "all your wonderful children and your wonderful husband" (*F.S.*, 91). Flattery of Jo's appearance, "You're much lovelier than your photo," leads directly to a major cause of her chagrin, the fact that her husband does not find her alluring any more. When the woman finally attacks, her method confirms the terminal constriction of her perspective: "What does your husband think of you, eh? Does he find you attractive? Eh, I've been wondering, do you think your husband would find me desirable? Eh?" (*F.S.*, 93). Far from assailing Jo as a person, the woman assails her *solely* as an object of male desire. The most potent weapon she can find to employ is Jo's presumed doubts about her continuing desirability.

Reviewers have argued that the comic sound and fury of this scene ultimately signify nothing. It is dismissed as "a Pinteresque" extravagance. Stanley Kauffmann finds it "totally irrelevant to the story."[32] Yet, in Pinter's conception, it is an integral part of the work as a whole. The strange woman both contributes to Jo's nightmare by subjecting her to unwarranted attack and, at the same time, presents her with a distorted reflection of her own dilemma. Pinter is careful to indicate in his directions for the scene that "*She is middle-aged*" (*F.S.*, 91). Each woman confronts the same fears: loss of beauty, the termination of the ability to conceive children, and insecurity over the affections of her husband. Pinter even invokes a direct parallel by referring back to her psychiatrist's suggestion that Jo cut down on liquids:

WOMAN: Oooh, I'm so thirsty.

Pause.

JO: Would you . . . like a cup of tea?

WOMAN: I'm off liquids. (*F.S.*, 92)

She cruelly reminds Jo of her husband's infidelity and anticipates her sterilization. But, this woman also presents her with a study in self-delusion, as she desperately clings to the tenuous threads of identity.

In his examination of the private world that an individual creates to protect herself, this scene is characteristic of the writer's early work. Examples abound. In *The Room*, Rose constructs her reality around the circumscribed space which is her cocoon: "No, this room's all right for me. I mean, you know where you are."[33] Visitors like Mr. Kidd or the Sands are regarded as potentially sinister threats to its integrity. Although the characters in *The Homecoming* are much more complex and sophisticated, they retain the same capacity for constructing their own idiosyncratic realities. Teddy, the professional metaphysician, lives according to his bankrupt concept of "intellectual equilibrium," while Lenny defines experience according to an equally inappropriate notion of himself as a homespun philosopher. Each of them is both protective and aggressively defensive, as when Teddy remarks, "You wouldn't understand my works. You wouldn't have the faintest idea of what they were about."[34]

Teddy, like the unnamed woman and Jo herself, affords his environment its particular meaning and hence is trapped by it. A seedy living-room, typical of a thousand seaside boardinghouses, becomes the setting in *The Birthday Party* for a bizarre celebration that ultimately destroys "the birthday boy." In *A Slight Ache*, the matchseller acts as a catalyst for Edward's fears. From pompous, but not extraordinary, social platitudes, he works himself gradually into a frenzy of abject terror:

> EDWARD: You *are* laughing. You're laughing. Your face. Your body. (*Overwhelming nausea and horror.*) Rocking . . . gasping . . . rocking . . . shaking . . . rocking . . . heaving . . . rocking. . . . You're laughing at me! Aaaaahhhh![35]

The scene at the hairdresser's parallels Pinter's early plays in its suggestion that everyday normality may conceal a dark world of threat and potential destruction.

Although Pinter might well argue that his aim was to render Mortimer's novel faithfully into a screenplay, the result is a unique and original work that owes a good deal more to him than to the novelist. The process of adaptation inevitably involves radical change. What is selected from the novel and the manner in which it is employed in its new context are both consequences of the adapter's response to the source. Even those elements that seem remarkably similar to material in the novel, of necessity, take on new significance in a different form. Where Mortimer's work is diffuse but explicit, Pinter's screenplay is economical but highly provocative. Where the narrator engages in a confessional examination of her own inadequacies, Pinter's Jo is positioned in a form that seeks to combine objective representation with subjective perspective. Consequently, we are often reminded that although we become spectators of important incidents in her life, the principle of organization, the selection of what is significant, is a product of her unique point of view. Scenes that Pinter develops from details which attract him in the novel take on a radically different meaning in the screenplay. They become part of Jo's nightmarish sense of increasing helplessness and impending doom in the face of overwhelming social subjugation. It is a crisis that succeeds her public breakdown in Harrods and it is much more debilitating than the breakdown. Indeed, it is so strong and effective that the supposed formal resolution of her dilemma at the end of the work seems somewhat overwhelmed by its power. The screenplay of *The Pumpkin Eater* represents the continuation of Pinter's concern in *The Servant* and in his early plays with the victim's partial responsibility for his or her own subjugation, inextricably intertwined with the cutthroat power struggles inherent in human interaction.

NOTES

1. Brendan Gill, "Drawbacks of Domesticity," *New Yorker*, November 14, 1964, p. 148.

2. John Coleman, "Pumpkin Pie," *New Statesman*, July 17, 1964, p. 97.

3. John Russell Taylor, *Harold Pinter* (London: Longmans, 1969), p. 20.

4. Arnold P. Hinchliffe, *Harold Pinter* (New York: Twayne, 1967), p. 134.

5. Quoted in Virginia Noyes, "Complex Compelling Chronicle of Human Foibles," *Chicago Tribune Magazine of Books*, April 21, 1963, p. 3.

6. Penelope Mortimer, *The Pumpkin Eater* (London: Hutchinson, 1962), pp. 55-57. (All subsequent quotations from this volume are indicated by the abbreviation *P.E.*).

7. Martin Esslin, *Pinter: A Study of His Plays* (London: Eyre Methuen, 1973), p. 195. Originally published as *The Peopled Wound* (London: Methuen, 1970).

8. Hichliffe, *Harold Pinter*, p. 135.

9. William Baker and Stephen Tabachnick, *Harold Pinter* (Edinburgh: Oliver and Boyd, 1973), p. 96.

10. Ernest Betts, "Angled for the Ladies," *People*, July 19, 1964, p. 7.

11. Baker and Tabachnick, *Harold Pinter*, p. 96.

12. Lawrence M. Bensky, "Harold Pinter: An Interview," *Paris Review*, X, 39 (1966): 18.

13. Olga Franklin, "Penelope Mortimer on the Problem of Marriage," *Daily Telegraph*, September 3, 1971, p. 11.

14. Marshall Pugh, "Trying to Pin Down Pinter," *Daily Mail*, March 7, 1964, p. 8.

15. Harold Pinter, *The Pumpkin Eater*, in *Five Screenplays* [*F.S.*] (London: Methurn, 1971), p. 106. All quotations from Pinter's screenplay are from this source.

16. "From Page to Screen," *Times Literary Supplement*, June 18, 1971, p. 695.

17. "Harold Pinter, Director," *Cinebill*, I, 7 (1974): 7. American Film Theatre Program for *Butley*.

18. Joseph Losey, "*The Servant*: Notes on the Film," p. 1.

19. "Be a Man, Mrs. Evans," *Times Literary Supplement*, October 5, 1962, p. 773.

20. Harold Pinter, "Speech: Hamburg 1970." *Theatre Quarterly*, I, 3 (1971): 3.

21. Harold Pinter, "Between the Lines." *Sunday Times Magazine*, March 4, 1962, p. 25. (Speech given at the Seventh National Student Drama Festival in Bristol.)

22. Ibid.

23. Harold Pinter, *The Collection and The Lover* (London: Methuen, 1963), p. 19.

24. Pinter, "Between the Lines," p. 25.

25. Pinter, *The Collection and The Lover*, p. 45.

26. Ibid.

27. Esslin, *Pinter: A Study of His Plays*, p. 195.

28. Baker and Tabachnick, *Harold Pinter*, p. 98.

29. Daniel Salem, "Les Adaptations cinématographiques de Pinter." *Etudes anglaises*, XXV, 4 (1966), p. 500.

30. John Sherwood, "Interview with Harold Pinter," BBC European Service, in the series "The Rising Generation," March 3, 1960. (Duplicated manuscript quoted by Martin Esslin, *Harold Pinter*, p. 36.)

31. Harold Pinter, *The Birthday Party* (London: Methuen, 1960), p. 87.

32. Stanley Kauffmann, "Early Winter Roundup," *New Republic*, December 19, 1964, p. 29.

33. Harold Pinter, *The Room and the Dumb Waiter* (London: Methuen, 1960), p. 8.

34. Harold Pinter, *The Homecoming* (London: Methuen, 1965), p. 61.

35. Harold Pinter, *Complete Works: One* (New York: Grove, 1977), p. 199.

FIGURE 2. *Accident.* Dirk Bogarde as Oxford don Stephen and Jacqueline Sassard as Francesca. United Artists Corporation. Jerry Ohlinger Archives.

CHAPTER TWO

⊞

The Eternal Summer of
Joseph Losey and Harold Pinter's
Accident

WHEELER WINSTON DIXON

Of all of Joseph Losey's films, I have always admired *Accident* (1967) the most, even when placed side-by-side with *The Servant* (1963) or *These Are the Damned* (1962), Losey's two other key works of the 1960s. *Accident* holds a claim on my memory by virtue of its timeless embrace of eternal youth and endless summers—what the artist Joseph Cornell referred to in one of his films as the *Centuries of June*. *Accident* moves in a world that is privileged, stillborn, insular, and sodden with alcohol; it is also a world of great beauty and sudden death, power and weakness, splendor and decay. The film represents an idyll, a high-water mark in the careers of Harold Pinter, who wrote the screenplay based on Nicholas Mosley's novel; of Joseph Losey, who brought Pinter and Mosley's vision to the screen; of the actors Dirk Bogarde, Stanley Baker, Jacqueline Sassard, Michael York, Vivien Merchant, Delphine Seyrig, Alexander Knox, and Freddie Jones, all of whom have seldom been seen to better advantage; of John Dankworth, whose cool, sparse score epitomizes the tranced-out self-assurance of 1960s British high society; and of Gerry Fisher, the brilliant cameraman whose later credits include *Mr. Klein* (1975), *Fedora* (1978),

Wise Blood (1979), and numerous other films, but who never surpassed his work on *Accident,* his first film as director of photography.

Shot "on location at Cobham, Oxford, London, Syon House, and Twickenham Studios [from July through] September 1966" (Milne, 189), *Accident* is a film of stasis and movement, celebrity and obscurity, clarity and internal chaos. It is also a film of supreme illusion; as Losey himself has observed, "all those summer scenes were shot in icy cold weather, and a lot of it was rain . . . we would often prepare a shot for some hours and then get forty-five seconds to shoot it; and if it wasn't right on the first take, there wasn't time to do another; and by the time there seemed to be enough exposure to get another take, the sun had moved so completely that all the lights had to be changed. So it took us days and days to get that stuff" (Milne, 113). Yet, this tedious process of perfectionism is precisely what lends the film its undeniable air of supreme, arrogant, delicious visual authority. Everything takes forever. The setups take forever, and the light is so fleeting that one can only count on a few minutes of precisely the right sunlight before the moment ineluctably slips away.

But it is in the essence of this process—capturing the same "forty-five seconds" of perfect light over and over again on successive days—that Losey found the inexorably unchanging visual universe ideal for Pinter's protagonists. More from Losey: "The overall texture of summer sunshine was very important, and very hard to get . . . the texture of sunlight, I think, is probably one of the most important [visual aspects of *Accident*], not just sunlight, but sunlight coming and going, clouds moving, obscuring the sun and then revealing it, and the different ways things look when they're in the sun and when they're not, when they're in darkness or not" (Milne, 112). Above all, the world of *Accident* is a world of light and the absence of light, of nights redolent with heat and torpor, and days of interminable beauty. Picnicking on the lawn, boating on the river, or ensconced in his rooms at Oxford, Stephen (Bogarde) is the sun-blessed intellectual who prefers to squander his days, and his talents, in pursuit of the ineffable—the dream of the eternal and immutable present. The world of *Accident* is summer, and the summer of *Accident* is the world entire for Stephen, Charley (Baker), Anna (Sassard), William (York), Rosalind (Merchant), and Francesca (Seyrig). One cannot imagine them existing in another universe. Like inverted vampires, they must live in the sun in order to exist. When they venture out at night, the results (as seen in the opening moments of the film) are usually disastrous.

It is altogether fitting that the two textual authors of *Accident* are present within the work, visually entombed in the world that they have helped to bring about. Nicholas Mosley, author of the novel, is seen briefly as an Oxford don; Pinter appears as Mr. Bell, a midlevel executive at the television network who Stephen so assiduously courts. Unquestionably, *Accident* is about celebrity, the creation of images to support the myth of celebrity, and the jettisoning of outmoded visual constructs that no longer appeal to the public or serve to propagate the myth of interchangeable celebrity. Jones, the "Frantic Man at [the] TV studio" is beside himself because he can feel his hold on the visual slipping away; Bell, seated behind him in the sleekly impersonal space of the studio exudes confidence, and sports a feral grin. Charley is a televisual celebrity. He discusses books, cultural trends, wears the proper glasses to give him a more forbiddingly "intellectual" look, and holds Stephen in contempt because Stephen is unable to command a similar position. Still, when Stephen tells Charley that he has "a meeting with *your* producer" during a particularly alcoholic and nasty supper at home, Charley is unnerved.

Charley is disposable, just as Jones's character has proven disposable, and perhaps, with some grooming, even Stephen can be tapped to replace him. Both men despise William as a shallow undergraduate whose chief attribute is the possession of a desirable girlfriend, Anna. During supper, William becomes hopelessly drunk as Charley and Stephen exchange taunts over the dinner table, brutally competing for the ownership of televisual space, of Anna, of a claim on William's naive admiration. And yet, both Stephen and Charley lack the one essential element that William possesses in shameless abundance: youth. William is blond, conventionally handsome, athletic, and can easily beat Stephen in physical contests (as he proves several times throughout the film). Both Charley and Stephen wish to possess William's youth, and with it his strength, so that they may in turn possess Anna, who admires the older men for their magisterial command of the academic world they all share. When William dies (at the beginning of the film; his presence is seen only in flashbacks,) he takes his youth with him, but he also takes the abstract ideas of hope and possibility, of the future (any future) with him to his grave. Eternally dead, William is also eternally young, possessed of a future which, though removed, still radiates promise.

Eternally alive, Charley and Stephen are also members of the society of the living dead; all hope, all sense of promise has been removed from their lives. They search for external validation (appearances on television, the possession of Anna) as proofs of their continued existence, but all that these empty pursuits accentuate is the bankruptcy of their stillborn nonexistence. Stephen and Charley have hit the glass ceiling of academe; they are afraid of scandal, afraid of reproof from the aging but implacable provost, afraid of their aging bodies, afraid of their inner vacuity. Their relationships are lies or competitions. Stephen is unfaithful to his wife Rosalind in the most casual manner, as if infidelity within marriage is both inevitable and ineffably boring. When Stephen meets Francesca in a shabby London restaurant and then returns to her flat, their thoughts are heard on the film's soundtrack, but they have no need to actually *speak* to each other. Whatever they might say would be utterly banal (as indeed it is), so why bother? Stephen and Charley both inhabit a world they no longer believe in. They simply go through the motions and repeat the required phrases, cite the appropriate texts. If, as F. Scott Fitzgerald observed, "action is character," by their assiduous non-action both Stephen and Charley *have* no character. All they possess is artifice, and even that is running out.

For both Losey and Pinter, initially collaboration was extremely difficult. Pinter's screenplay for Losey's *The Servant* (1963) was their first work together; Losey noted that on that film Pinter had

> already written a screenplay which I thought was 75 percent bad and unproducible, but had a number of scenes which were not changed as they reached the screen. I gave him a very long list of rewrites which enraged him, and we had an almost disastrous first session. He said he was not accustomed to being worked with this way—neither was I, for that matter—but he came to see me the next day, I tore up the notes, and we started through the script. (Milne, 152)

By the time of *Accident*, the writer and director were working together much more smoothly:

> With Harold now [in 1967], it's a question of detailed discussion of intent; then he usually writes a first draft, which I comment on, and which he then rewrites; and there may or may not be small rewrites during the course of shooting—more often than not there aren't. I may ask for additions, there may be tiny things within a scene— [and] he's very often around during shooting. (Milne, 152–53)

Pinter was indeed "around" during the lengthy production of *Accident*.

Casting was also difficult. Bogarde and Baker had both worked with Losey before but were perceived by the public as widely divergent cinematic types—Bogarde the repressed intellectual of *The Servant*, Baker the rough-and-tumble man of action in Losey's peculiar and atmospheric prison drama *The Criminal* (1960). The casting of Baker as an Oxford don, successful novelist, and television personality surprised many of Losey's intimates, although in retrospect Baker was the perfect choice to play against Bogarde's mild-mannered, yet intensely pressurized persona. Losey commented after *Accident* opened that "I thought the combination of Dirk Bogarde and Stanley Baker was a very good one, and it was one which was ultimately financible, although with great difficulty. Also because I knew from several pictures, in each of which the performances are quite different, that Baker could do it. I always go with actors on feel, not on what they have done" (Milne, 165). Baker was, of course, delighted for a chance to play slightly against type (the thick eyeglasses helped, to a degree, in the transformation of his iconic presence), but what Losey was banking on was Baker's hyperaggressive sexuality spilling over into Bogarde's performance area, providing Bogarde with a presence of raw physicality to respond to (something that James Fox couldn't provide in *The Servant*). In this film, precisely because he has so many confrontations with Baker, Bogarde discards his usual mask of passive acquiescence on a number of memorable occasions (the dinner table scene being one), to create a new and more charged persona, seething with frustration and barely controlled violence.

As Losey noted, the visual look of the film achieved by Fisher was the result of a good deal of patience and hard labor; it is also worth noting that Fisher was not his first choice as director of photography. "I couldn't get Douglas Slocombe," Losey told an interviewer, "who was my first choice . . . I couldn't get Chris Challis. Gerry Fisher had been my [camera] operator on *Modesty Blaise* [1966], and I liked the way he worked. I gave him three days to decide whether he wanted to try as a lighting cameraman, whether he could, and told him if he said he could, I would accept him. In somewhat less than three days he said he could, and did, and he's done a brilliant job" (Milne, 159). So both in front of the camera and behind the camera, *Accident* was itself the product of a series of fortuitous acts of random chance and suggestion, but perhaps none so magically transcendent as the circumstances surrounding the scene between Stephen and Francesca.

Losey had decided that the scene between Stephen and Francesca, shot for the most part in a dingy restaurant (whose decor is dominated by a sign reading "Eat Your Meals Here and Keep the Wife as a Pet") should be silent, with their thoughts heard on a voice-over soundtrack and the actors' lips never moving on the screen. Losey recalled that "this happened partly because Delphine Seyrig was enormously busy and expensive and I got her to play the role on the basis of spending two days shooting in England. She came over on a Friday, we read and rehearsed, we shot the restaurant on Sunday, and the scene in the flat on Monday . . . she was gone before we saw the rushes on Tuesday" (Milne, 115, 117). When "laying in" the voice over the silent shots, Losey discovered that although both actors had been instructed not to speak, they were making the tiniest, involuntary lip movements anyway, giving the viewer the suggestion that the characters are about to speak, but are too embarrassed to do so; or alternatively, and less poetically, that the scene is unintentionally "out-of-synch" (Milne, 117). Although these slight stirrings of the actors' lips are somewhat unnerving, and certainly unplanned, they do impart to the audience a sense of tension, failed communication, and unspoken desire, which is precisely the territory surveyed in *Accident*.

As one might expect, Pinter's use of dialogue in *Accident* is spare and minimal. In the opening minutes of the film, there is no dialogue at all, just the natural sounds of the English countryside at night, almost immediately punctuated by "a sudden screech, grind, smash and splintering" as the car carrying William and Anna crashes (Pinter, 219). Stephen investigates; his first line of dialogue is a single word, as he stares down into the wreckage of the car at William's lifeless body. "William?" he asks (Pinter, 221). As Anna emerges from the wreckage, Stephen suddenly screams, "Don't! You're standing on his face!" (Pinter, 222). Transfixed as if in a dream, Anna and Stephen stand next to the car, staring at each other. Stephen scoops Anna up and deposits her by the side of the road. Through the next few scenes, as he escorts Anna back to his house, there is very little said at all, and all of the dialogue belongs to Stephen. Anna remains mute, expressionless, stunned by the tragedy that has befallen her. Only when the police arrive to investigate the car crash does Pinter's dialogue take on the "normal" cadences of speech, and even here, the interrogation sequence is surreal, phantasmal.

As the film progresses, Pinter cuts from a mini-flashback of "Anna's shoe, standing, digging into William's face" (Pinter, 228) to Stephen's rooms at Oxford, where Stephen and William obviously are further in the past) exchange mildly confrontational ripostes under the pretext of a tutorial session. The real object of discussion is Anna, "Anna von Graz und Leoben" (Pinter, 229). Stephen is clearly taken with Anna, William is

smitten with Anna, Stephen's wife Rosalind (in a domestic scene following this one, Pinter, 232–33) is clearly threatened by Anna, and Charley
pursues Anna with arrogant and transparent lust. A long weekend at
Stephen's house brings all of these contradictory passions to a boil and
transforms the serene British countryside into a metaphoric and physical
battlefield, as in the tennis game between Charley, Anna, William, and
Stephen described in Pinter (245). The brutal game of medicine ball
between William and Stephen and an assorted group of jaded, male aristocrats proceeds entirely without dialogue (as does the tennis game) in
Pinter's script (270–72).

Within the world of *Accident*, all is a contest. Manners merely cover
up the savagery that lurks underneath the manicured surface. Within the
context of this world of endless trials and rematches, William's death
comes almost as a relief, because only death can take him out of play, out
of jeopardy. By the conclusion of the film, in which Anna dumps Charley
after their brief relationship (much to Stephen's ill-concealed delight), we
have come to feel as trapped within Losey and Pinter's world as the protagonists of *Accident*. And at the very end of the film, as Stephen gathers
up his children, Ted and Clarissa, and takes them back into the house
under a dazzling sun, there is no sound at all except for a replay of the car
crash that opened the film (Pinter, 284), directly indicating that the only
escape from this hell of class privilege is death, and an ignominious death
at that. None of the characters in the film derives any satisfaction out of
his or her existence, with the possible exception of Anna (when she
escapes from Charley's possessive clutches [Pinter, 281–82]). Nonetheless,
all of Pinter and Losey's characters will continue to play out their parts,
silhouetted against a serene, bucolic landscape, a landscape of surface
beauty and internal, ceaseless corruption.

Losey's visual style in bringing Mosley and Pinter's world to the
screen is a study in contrasts. In some sequences, particularly the dreamy
boat ride during which Stephen covets Anna while William poles along
the canal, Losey changes camera positions with alacrity, framing Anna's
legs, Stephen's crossed arms, William's pole refracted on the surface of the
water, the figure of a swan unfurling its feathers with nonchalant ease.
Supplemented by Dankworth's jazz-inspired score for woodwinds and
harp, the sequence effortlessly captures the rarefied atmosphere of
academe at play. In opposition to this, during the kitchen sequence
directly after Stephen's meeting with Francesca, Losey's camera runs for
nearly six minutes without a break. In this lengthy scene, Stephen makes

himself some scrambled eggs while Charley reads a "confidential" letter from his estranged wife, Laura (who has written to Stephen), asking for Stephen's help in patching up their troubled marriage. The exteriors of the film are flooded with sunlight, but the interiors are drab and almost colorless, an effect that Losey admitted that he was striving for.

In an interview with Tom Milne, Losey noted that "on the interiors of the house, and also the colleges, the effort was primarily to remove colour, or at least colour that would be at all obtrusive; and at the same time to get cluttered interiors that were not purposeless, giving an overall sense of disorder" (Milne, 112). Stephen's isolated country house is a tangle of narrow stairs and warren-like rooms, offering neither comfort or any sense of real domesticity. Enormous amounts of alcohol are consumed throughout the film, ostensibly to blot out the emptiness of the character's lives, but to no avail. As with Stephen's brief fling with Francesca, ("a real lost night, which instead of relieving frustration, makes it worse," as Losey observed [Milne, 117]), the endless scotch and lager consumed by Stephen, William, and Charley bring them no solace. Significantly, Anna and Rosalind refrain from overindulgence.

Rosalind has a compelling reason for not drinking: she is expecting (with a good deal of stoic apprehension) the birth of their third child. Anna doesn't drink to excess because she wants to remain in control. Although superficially the film seems to center on three men lusting after Anna, in actuality the narrative of *Accident* is a demonstration of Anna's dominance of the social milieu that the members of the group inhabit. During the previously described sequence in Stephen's kitchen, when Charley orders Anna to "get the letter" that his wife has written Stephen, Anna makes no response of any kind, forcing Charley to retrieve the letter himself. Although Anna offers to cook Stephen's eggs for him in the same scene, she is not the endlessly domestic drudge that Rosalind has allowed herself to become. One might forcefully argue that *Accident*, in its own primitive 1960s fashion, is to some degree a feminist statement. Just as the protagonist of Chantal Akerman's more recent *Night and Day* (1991) abruptly and wordlessly leaves both of her lovers behind in that film's final moments, so Anna decides at the conclusion of *Accident* that she has extracted all that she cares to from either Stephen or Charley and leaves Oxford for her home in Austria. This she does with the same sort of cool detachment that the character of Julie displays in Akerman's film; Charley's entreaties are powerless to hold her, and Stephen understands implicitly that "there's nothing to keep her here" (Pinter, 282).

The only clear "loser" in *Accident* is William, the young aristocrat who was "made to be . . . slaughtered" (Pinter, 237), as Stephen notes in his rooms near the start of the film. During the brutal game of medicine ball at Lord Codrington's house between William, Stephen, and the other quests, Stephen reminds William of his mortality and his class. "Isn't it true that all aristocrats want to die?" asks Stephen. "I don't" William promptly responds (Pinter, 270), but both references are far too ominous to be taken lightly. William is doomed precisely because he is too beautiful, too rich, too much in love with Anna, too dependent upon others for the knowledge that he alone must gain through practical experience. Losey frames William throughout the film in a series of Christ-like close-ups, underscoring his imminent martyrdom, and yet for all of that, the viewer finds it hard to work up much sympathy for William. He is simply too naive.

Rosalind keeps her eyes shut to that which she does not wish to know, and Charles and Stephen behave like rapacious animals, satisfying their appetites of the moment without any regard for possible future consequences. Even after the car accident in which William is killed and Anna rendered momentarily passive and semicatatonic, Stephen, after disposing of the policemen and their routine inquiries, can't restrain himself from raping Anna (Pinter, 274–77) in the bedroom of his home, while William's body is presumable on its way to the morgue. Stephen and Charley are absolute monsters, and they know it. They accept their living damnation with a certain amount of panache and style, even if that doesn't for a moment excuse their actions. Stephen's children are innocent bystanders in all of this, barely packed away to "Granny's . . . for three weeks" (Pinter, 244) by the time matters have come to a head. Rosalind has implicitly agreed to live with the horrific situation that she has helped to create through her indifference, and she has given up any hope of real communication with anyone. If it is impossible to feel sympathetic for any of the film's protagonists, then Anna emerges as the narrative's victor by default, simply for having the presence of mind to flee from an impossible situation.

The sexual ethics of the 1960s are everywhere apparent in *Accident*: blatant infidelity is routinely condoned, no one seems to use any sort of contraceptives, and the issue of sexually transmitted diseases is never broached (at the time, of course, AIDS did not exist). For all of the characters' moral squalor, Losey finds the twilight world inhabited by Pinter and Mosley's creations both sensuous and sinisterly seductive. The endless days of leisure at Oxford must naturally give way to a harsher reality in time, but in the static world of *Accident*, that day of reckoning exists in the dim and distant future, if at all. There is the sense throughout the film that one can play a seemingly endless series of highly dangerous games and still get away with it because the safety nets of wealth, tenure, and class are firmly in place and will scoop up anyone unlucky enough to make a potentially fatal misstep.

Near the end of the film, after Stephen's rape of Anna in his home, Stephen receives word by telephone of the birth of his third child, on the morning after William's death. Already, Stephen has begun to move Anna out his life ("right . . . your handbag" [Pinter, 277]) so that Rosalind and the children can return. In his own view of events, Stephen has "scored" over Charley—he has taken Anna against her will, and it seems he will get away with it. As the dawn breaks over the university, Stephen helps Anna over the Oxford dormitory wall ("no one must see you" [Pinter, 278]), implicitly demanding Anna's silence in exchange for his silence about the still-murky details of the fatal road accident. To all of this Anna acquiesces. Stephen has too much power. In the final sequence in Stephen's rooms at Oxford, Charley, superficially shocked by William's death, still has the arrogance to believe that Anna will stay with him. Stephen knows better. In the exchanges of power that form the narrative of *Accident*, Anna has been a victim and a participant at the same time, the kind of moral (or amoral) multivalency that infuriates those who wish for clear-cut solutions to the vicissitudes of existence.

Where, then, is the real location of power in *Accident*? At what point does the narrative focus become fixed? At what juncture are we able to clearly discern the motives and values of the characters we have just spent 105 minutes with, as the final end credits for the film appear on the screen? I would submit that the struggle for power that informs the narrative of *Accident* implicates every one of the film's protagonists, even William (who is clearly seen as "too good" to survive in a world comprised of lies, subterfuge, and elaborate deceptions). The world of *Accident* is a world of fatal and continual moral compromise in which every character is guilty of some sort of manipulation and/or vanity, and no one is entirely free of blame. Most critical analysis of *Accident* has focused on William, Charley, and Stephen and their ostensible midlife crises as the central focal points of the text.

I would submit instead that the central focus of the film is the visual and tactile world which its denizens inhabit, a domain of summer sun and shade, drab interiors, freshly cut lawns, and genteelly shabby university libraries. As I read it, Pinter, Losey, and Mosley are saying that this environment of endless power and prestige has fatally compromised all of the participants in *Accident*. Anna may escape, but she will not escape unscathed. To say nothing of the trauma of William's death, she will carry the humiliation and anger of her rape by Stephen with her for the rest of her life, while Stephen and Charley will embark upon yet another round of senseless infidelities as Rosalind and Laura look the other way. Life will go on. New students will arrive to be schooled by Charles and Stephen, but they will find to their dismay that the lessons which they have to learn are very harsh indeed.

If the world of *Accident* is alluring and romantic in a decadent, excessive fashion, something like a fantasy of Lautréamont or Rimbaud, it is also a domain of endless, circular pain (witness the repeated car crash) and disappointment. Losey and Pinter have contrived to make this world real and immediate to us, but even as we are seduced by the luxurious aimlessness of *Accident*, the film's final frames serve as a warning. This picture-perfect world is a gigantic and alluring deception, and we would be well-advised not to be taken in. Even for a few hours, to live in the suffocatingly perfect world of *Accident* is a trial. Imagine, then, what it must be like to live there for an eternity.

FIGURE 3. *The Go-Between*. Dominic Guard as the young Leo and Julie Christie as Marian. Columbia Pictures. Jerry Ohlinger Archives.

CHAPTER THREE

---------------------- ⊞ ----------------------

The Ecology of The Go-Between

MARYA BEDNERIK

In 1971, the film version of Harold Pinter's screenplay *The Go-Between,* an adaptation of L. P. Hartley's 1953 award-winning novel directed by Joseph Losey, won the acclaimed Palme d'Or award at the Cannes Film Festival. During the eight years of preparation, which eventuated in winning the "golden palm frond," the ecological revolution of the 1960s symbolized its importance by declaring the first Earth Day. Issues of the survival of the planet and the well-being of other species captured the public's attention (Sessions, xi). Ecology is a "biological science concerned with studying the relation of organisms, species, and communities of species to each other and to their environment (Sessions, 265)."

Poets and artists from the earliest times have explored such relationships in images and themes. In a critical study written within the same time frame as the Pinter-Losey project, Joseph W. Meeker argues for the importance of investigation through the study of literature as an influential repository for ecological images, interests, and ideologies. Writers both consciously and unconsciously in various formats posit a connection between people and the planet, which when studied reveal an ecological bias. Meeker speaks to the importance of such critical studies: "Ecological disaster promised to undermine human life and perhaps the conditions required by all life, not merely this or that political state, ideology, or religious tradition (5)." In his response to the problems of the planet, Meeker argues the need for this kind of study of biological themes and relationships which appear in literary works in an attempt to discover what roles have been played by literature in the ecology of the human species (9). As the environmental movement progressed historically, a group of academics calling themselves Ecocritics formed the Association for the Study of Literature and the Environment and held their first meeting in the summer of l995. In her *Ecologies of Theater* (1996), Bonnie Marranca argues for "the recognition of an ecosystem as part of a cultural system and of natural history as inseparable from the history of the world" (xiv).

This Pinter-Losey collaboration makes an interesting site for a reading of culture and landscapes. In the realization of content and form, the film—true to its title—takes the spectator in a search for meanings through timespace between many polarities on a journey between childhood and adulthood, nature and civilization, mythology and reality, aristocratic and lower classes, male and female, self and other, past and present, commerce and art, and the nineteenth and twentieth centuries. Although Pinter has frequently expressed interests in crossing such thresholds, often his locations on the stagescape are limited to a single room designed with minimalistic power. The film medium, however, requires that scenes expand outward into many timespaces, and the screenplay provides unusual freedoms of movement for the playwright. The closeness of the collaboration between this writer and director has been well-established. In interviews with Pinter and with Losey, each identifies and admits to the success of intuitive and like-mindedness of the other in the representation of the work. In the screenplay, Pinter meticulously locates the shot sequences and content to be presented by Losey with his production designer. Unlike Pinter's plays for the theatre, the film script demands that its energies move outward. Conversely, the theatre confines its energy within the space of representation; there the dramatist has capitalized on its intensity with a single interior scene design. Unlike his plays, often in this film Pinter can foreground in single frames devoid of humans the concepts of plant, tree, field, stream, lawn, garden, road, village, farm, cathedral, and country house. Its central character, Leo, crosses numerous boundaries in his role as go-between.

The film also is an important site for a critical view of Pinter attitudes toward ethology. His verbal images of animal behavior and territory as metaphors in some of his scenes in the film become a present-day bestiary. Horses, a deer herd, flies, geese, and one dog are shown in single shots and their meanings defined or redefined in their juxtapositions to human activities. Thus, *The Go-Between* presents an excellent opportunity to investigate the implications of Pinter's ecological and ethological statements represented visually and verbally. Marranca calls for critics to consider the linkage between the world of artistic representation and its environment, connecting it to and investigating that world as part of a greater cultural aesthetic system. Pinter's interests in politics have been well-established; his interests as an environmentalist have not. Still, as Meeker writes,:

> Philosophical ideas defining the relationship between man and nature are often expressed or implied in literary works, revealing a history of human beliefs concerning the meaning of natural processes and also revealing the cultural ideologies which have contributed to our contemporary ecological crisis. Most important, literary ecology makes it possible for us to study the function of literary art as it influences the survival of the human species. (10)

Pinter writes as an environmentalist in *The Go-Between*. It is revealing, then, to focus on how geography and climate serve as emblems in the work. What is the relationship among humans, animals, plants, place, and the planet? How are these interdependencies expressed on page and screen? What does Pinter praise or blame?

As guest and messenger, Leo the errand boy travels over unfamiliar grounds as he facilitates an improper love affair between members of two social classes. The romantic liaison between the aristocratic Marian and the tenant farmer Ted Burgess serves as the central reflector for foregrounding the story of Leo's coming of age. An archive in the form of a diary kept by the young Leo triggers the investigations of potent images of a summer past made present and now reread by the adult Leo. These reminiscences occur in voice-overs and often in scenes that predict and implicate the past event in future actions. Pinter's selection of the happenings that compose the shooting script for the film are precisely selected and emphasize the importance of locations that serve as signs.

In recounting the writing process, Pinter expresses to Losey frustration and blockage in his initial efforts to capture the essence of the novel, called by critics a minor masterpiece. Losey responds by advising Pinter just to begin. Hartley's autobiographical novel (1952) fictionalizes his experiences as a schoolboy invited by a chum to spend a summer vacation with him at the friend's estate home. Set in memory, in the story an adult Leo recounts a past incident that has shaped his present character. When asked about the origins of his fiction, the novelist claims to remember three important things. From the natural and physical world of that summer he recalls only the double staircase, the cedar tree in the garden, and the deadly nightshade in an outbuilding.

These three environmental images, made important through repetition in Pinter's film script, provide interesting emblems of the tension in the world. The horseshoe staircase is frequently shown. Stairs are the perfect metaphor of change and transition. As an image, their meanings are buried deep in human consciousness. From Genesis' Jacob with his dream of angels climbing ladders to heaven to those cinematic frames burned into the retina of the eye of Rhett Butler carrying Scarlett O'Hara up the grand flight of stairs in *Gone With The Wind* or Fred Astaire (whose name contains the perfect pun) dancing down them in many of his movies or to nursery rhymes where Christopher Robin sits halfway down or "As I was going up the stair / I met a man who wasn't there," stairs have resided as powerful archetypes in the collective unconscious. For the Victorian household, they implied social direction similarly captured in the memorable *Masterpiece Theatre* series *Upstairs, Downstairs*.

Symbolically, Pinter locates the outsider Leo's climb and descent into assimilation through assigned tasks and placement within the culture of the family, whose customs and values are those of an aristocratic old order. The schoolboys occupy a bedroom on the top floor away from the adult world. Shortly after their arrival at his home, Leo's friend gets the measles and Leo the neophyte is removed to yet a more separate and distant bedroom. To explore the geography of the house or to move into the places inhabited by the adults, Leo must go up or down these stairs. Sometimes they become the raceway for childhood contests with his friend to see who can get to the top or the bottom first. As Leo moves between the lower and upper regions of the house, he passes portraits of the ancestors on the wall and servants treading up and down engaged in carrying out their assigned duties. These stairs are a physical representation of the transition that the adolescent Leo makes from his liminal state to that of the liminoid place of his adulthood. In the film the spectator is taken into these two conditions in its shifts of timespace between the present and grown-up Leo, often absent from the screen but present as an aural icon. His voice is superimposed over visual images of the younger self engaged in the important events of that summer visit. Pinter cuts back and forth in time between the older Leo in the present retracing his past and the former Leo at a crucial intersection in achieving his manhood. The disunity of the displacements and ruptures in time creates the alignment of form with content that renders the novel differently and freshly into film. It no longer supports, in either form or content, Darwinian ideas of progress through the evolution of the species.

Hartley's remembered tree also is important in Pinter's retelling. It becomes transformed from cedar to oak and replaced from garden to a midpoint between manor house and its tenant's farmhouse. The tree serves as a way station on Leo the messenger's route from estate to farm. Here he rests and learns by opening the note that Marian loves another man and that he is implicit in facilitating the improper affair. As the carrier of a secret, Leo is both burdened and simultaneously empowered by this new knowledge. Sissela Bok's investigation into secrecy and moral choice suggests that "concepts of sacredness, intimacy, prayer, silence, prohibition, furtiveness, and deception influence the way we think about secrecy" (6). The treasure-burden of the secret and Leo's development of conflicting, multiple loyalties to Marian, whom he adores, and to her betrothed Viscount Trimingham, whom he admires, and to her lower-class lover Ted, whom he considers a friend and makes into a kind of father figure, cause Leo to betray them all.

The climate, with its rising temperature and the weather with its frequently overcast skies and rain, called for by the script and represented on the screen, function as emotional counterparts to the plot's events. Marian has used the heat of summer as an excuse to take Leo to the village to shop for a new suit. There, under the guise of propriety, she can meet her lover. It is in this green suit, a metaphoric uniform presented to her cavalier, that Leo is dressed at the moment of his discovery of the content of those notes that he carries. The relationship between Leo, the suit, and tree set the image in the mythological and magical realms. First, Leo is pictured standing on a chair showing off his new suit to a circle of admiring family members. There he is given a new name:

DENYS: What green is this?

MARIAN: Lincoln green.

DENYS: I thought so. I shall dub you Sir Robin Hood. (298)

There are, of course, many prophetic resonances in this renaming. The figure of Robin Hood, famous for taking from the rich and giving to the poor, connects also mythologically to the figure of the Green Man. According to William Anderson in *The Green Man,* this archetype of nature is prevalent throughout human history; he is variously represented in architecture, art, and literature. He signals the creative, fruitful spirit found in nature. This powerful source frequently formed as a mask with hairlike vegetation flowing from it also offers ties to the theatrical arts:

> The Green Man is the guardian and revealer of mysteries. In his mask form he is linked to the universal significance of the mask which are those of a part in a drama to be taken up and dropped again and of the world of spirits and of what lies behind death . . . he speaks of the mysteries of creation in time, of the hidden sources of inspiration, and of the dark nothingness out of which we come and to which we return. (33)

Whether Robin Hood and his famous tree of Sherwood Forest and his original connections to this archetype are conscious or unconscious in the screenwriter's mind, the image, like that of the stairs, resonates for humankind. In reference to the mysteries and in the ability to recall past memories, Anderson notes the relationship in "the ecstatic joy and release of the Dionysiac festivities" (162). With his connections to worship in the theatre's festive rites as well as being a god associated with death, Dionysus makes an appropriate figure for Pinter, who is the consummate man of theatrical imagination. Anderson quotes Samuel Taylor Coleridge's connection of the concept of imagination linked to the concept of self-knowledge:

> The Green Man is the threshold of the imagination between our outer natures and our deepest selves. . . . The Green Man then adapted to the changing attitude to Nature of the onlooker, awareness brought about by the growth of western science and technology. This stage of awareness . . . is reaching the end of its dominance. (163–64)

Similarly, there are symbolic connections with Hartley's third reminiscence, that of the deadly nightshade. This plant can remind the viewer subconsciously of the biblical presence of evil in the paradisiacal Garden of Eden. The deadly nightshade in the film is a lushly growing plant and is associated with both Marian and the boy. She is first seen lying in a hammock; then her image is displaced by that of the plant's. Pinter specifies: "it is a large glossy shrub with bell-shaped flowers. . . . The camera goes before them and stops, regarding the shrub" (289). In "Re-viewing Losey-Pinter," Edward T. Jones connects the line about Marian's beauty with the literal meaning of the plant's Latin name (belladonna). Leo wears a large, floppy hat which is also shaped like the flower. The belladonna stands in the corner of an old and unkept garden where in the disused outbuildings Marian and Ted later are discovered in the midst of their lovemaking. The magical and deadly nightshade is an important part of Leo's ritual exorcism. He mixes a potion from it, and eventually he pulls the plant frantically out of the ground.

Leo's initiation into the social structures of upper-class British culture takes place away from the locales of untamed or uncared for out-of-doors in a series of what Michel Foucault calls epistemological acts and transformations. In *The Archaeology of Knowledge,* Foucault notes that those acts which create and transverse their own thresholds "suspend the continuous accumulation of knowledge, interrupt its slow development and force it to enter a new time, cut if off from its empirical origin and its original motivations, cleanse it of its imaginary complicities. In so doing, the spectator is directed toward a search for a new type of rationality and its various effects" (4). Three places where important transformations occur and which shift the characters' understanding in the light of new information also shift the viewers' perception of the relationships between humans and land: the croquet lawn, the cricket pavilion, and the corn field—each natural territory was changed by humans for their own pleasure and use. These key spots place the Western humanist attitude toward the superiority of man in his separateness from nature.

Arriving as an initiate to the adult world of Brandham Hall, Leo's first view of the grown-up world is that of adults at play. Stopping on the stairs, Leo looks out from the stately manor house situated above a manicured lawn to where the Maudsleys are playing croquet. The selection of this popular Victorian social game is perfect, for "Croquet is a game of position and a player's ability to maneuver the others" (Osborn, 118). It is an excellent chronotope not only for suggesting the time period but also for signaling the social relationships to be developed by the film. The landscape, space carefully laid out and separated from the woods and the fields of Leo's messenger route, contrasts that use of nature, and the game whose rules are man-made reinforces the hierarchy in which man places self above and as controller of the natural world. The rigid rules of the social contest exemplified by croquet, which is often played in pairs, symbolically stand for the macrocosm of the older order. The boundaries of class make Marian's love for her tenant farmer an impossible permanent alliance. The croquet lawn tames and puts to use nature for human pleasure; it contrasts with the natural spaces of the woods that the errand causes him to pass. Leo's crossing from one geographical space to another also implies a change in social status. Marking his progression from innocence to the sexual knowledge that defines manhood, Leo moves through the larger world of the village, explores a cathedral, and returns to the manor house for a climactic move into the men's smoking room. There he learns about honor and that the woman who is the cause of a duel is never at fault.

At one point, wearing his green suit and having accepted the new role of messenger, Leo meets the Viscount Trimingham in the middle of the croquet lawn. Pinter comments ironically on the demise of the aristocracy and the state of nature:

> TRIMINGHAM: Trying to sneak past in dead ground.
>
> (*pause*)
>
> Where were you off to?
>
> LEW: Nowhere. (316)

Trimingham instructs Leo to bring Marian back "dead or alive." She is needed to complete a foursome in the croquet match. When Leo carries out these instructions, Marian asks jokingly, "Which is it? Am I dead or alive?" It is the survival of the species with which evolution is concerned, and it is Leo's compelling motive to find out the secret of its procreation. At the end of the movie, it is apparent that he has failed in his quest for knowledge—or he has been paralyzed by what he learned. He is described as "dried up"; he is without passion, dead inside.

Against another environment, which has been laid out for man's leisure, is the cricket pavilion. Crossing this boundary, Leo is situated on a metaphoric battlefield where he must take sides. The annual battle between the gentry and the village occurs here, and Leo is awarded a place on the gentry's team as its twelfth man (twelve is also Leo's age). In *From Ritual to Theatre*, Victor Turner points out that "Leisure can be conceived of as a betwixt-and-between, a neither-this-nor-that domain between two spells of work or between occupational and familial and civic activity" (40). He further defines leisure as the "freedom to generate new, symbolic worlds" (37). Leo, transformed in another change of clothing, instructed not to wear his school cap, is moved up in the social order. This annual cricket match between the two classes reinforces this differentiation, which also separates the lovers. Ted is known as a strong hitter and must be gotten out. Amusing sexual overtones are present as the cricket ball almost hits Marian. Leo's part in the game foreshadows his part in their betrayal as he makes the winning catch that knocks Ted out:

> LEO: I didn't really mean to catch you out.
>
> TED: It was a damn good catch. . . . I never thought I'd be caught out by our postman. (Pinter, 330)

Pinter describes Marian's physical response to this moment as being still with head bent. That is the gesture signaling both submission and prayer. The match suggests warfare between the classes and the importance of winning in order to maintain the honor of the upper class. The random act of Leo's important catch indicates the absurdity and randomness in the design of the universe. Like the dead ground of the croquet field, nothingness is at the center of the universe.

The screenwriter gets a lot of playful, metaphorical mileage from the selection of this game as well as the opportunity to indulge his passion for his favorite sport. The character information also contains ritual motifs of death and renewal. Mr. Maudsley, the old patriarch, is portrayed as no longer strong. His oldest son keeps the father in place; he does not allow him to run. Similarly, there are biblical allusions that compare Leo's act to that of David, who slew the giant. In Mel Gussow's interviews with Pinter, the playwright is quoted as saying that in his own value system he places cricket alongside his passions for his family and the theatre (25). Losey, who doesn't share Pinter's love of this game, confesses to identifying with the spectator whom he directed to yawn! (The distributors wanted the sequence cut claiming no one wanted to see a cricket match. However, according to Losey, even Americans unschooled in the game still found it amusing.)

The match demonstrates the nineteenth-century emphasis on equating athletic excellence with character. Pinter uses the game to define the characters and to predict the ending of his screenplay. Henry Newbolt in *Sports in the Movies* writes, "Cricket, like chess, is a game for the contemplative, something not easily transferable to the screen. It appears more often as necessary adjunct to the creation of an English atmosphere" (112). He notes that in movies cricket and rugby most frequently function as shorthand to perpetuate the concepts of sport as the means to manliness and virtue and self-knowledge.

After the victory, the victor/victim Leo learns the shattering piece of information that causes him to choose between sides represented once again by the fiancé and the lover. Marian is engaged to marry Viscount Trimingham. Leo's loyalties are torn. He is caught in the web of his infatuation with Marian and his admiration for Trimingham, whom he thinks can teach him about honor, and his liking for the father figure, Ted, whom he thinks can instruct him in the art of love. Ted has promised to provide the sexual information that Leo seeks in return for Leo's services as go-between. Cricket as a sign exemplifies in its complex and strict rules and in its particularized boundaries the social world into which Leo is being initiated.

Just as the mythological motif of the patriarch is present in this match, the farmer/lover whom Leo will betray is cinematically displaced by an implied image of James Frazer's corn king. Leo crosses once again through forest and field to find Ted, from whom he will collect the promised information and to whom he will bid farewell. Leo has decided to stop carrying messages. Symbolically, Ted is riding a huge threshing machine when Leo finds him. The crossing of thresholds and the mythological references not only result in new knowledge for the character and viewer but also in an added temporal dimension—a move to sacred time. Turner points out that in rites of passage the initiates "have been ritually prepared for a whole series of changes in the nature of the cultural and ecological activities to be undertaken" (95). The geographical movement cited by Turner is part of the change in status before the return to a "new, relatively stable, well-defined position in the total society" (94). Much of the power of the film to engage the spectator lies in these transformations, the crossings and counter-crossings with their mythological implications that transport the view to Turner's sacred time.

And, it is the subject of self-knowledge and identity with which Pinter is centrally concerned in this film. To progress to adulthood, Leo must gain new knowledge. From Ted he wants to know what love is; from Trimingham he wants a definition of honor. In return for delivering the lovers' notes, Leo has extracted a commitment from Ted to answer questions about "spooning," the childish but only word that he knows for the sexual act which is the line of demarcation between childhood innocence and adult experience:

LEO: You can't break your promise.

(*pause*)

TED: Well . . . it means putting your arm round a girl, and kissing her. That's what it means.

Leo jumping out of chair.

LEO: I know that! But it's something else too. It makes you *feel* something. (339)

Ted searches for an appropriate explanation:

TED: It's like whatever you like doing best, and then some more.

Close-up of Leo.

LEO: Yes, but *what more?* What is lover-like? What does it mean? What is a lover? What does a lover do? Are you a lover? What do you do? You know. I know you know. And I won't take any more messages for you unless you tell me! (340)

From the linear novel with its present-day prologue and epilogue and its emphasis on heredity and environment as the causal factors in the formation of identity, Pinter's cinematic reconstruction with its use of flashforwards and multiple viewpoints changes the novel's Aristotlean structure, which demonstrates a deterministic view of character. Pinter shifts away from the tenets of naturalism in which heredity and environment are the major factors in constructing character into a quantum universe where identity is a series of assigned roles. Pinter says, "I think I'm more conscious of a kind of ever-present quality in life . . . I certainly feel more and more that the past is not past, that it never was past. It's present" (quoted in Houston and Kinder, 198). Pinter tells Mel Gussow, "The whole question of time and all its reverberations and possible meanings really does seem to absorb me more and more" (209). The shifting away from psychologically developed characterization focuses attention on the broader social implications and forces a restructuring of perception. Through the mythological motifs and the disunity and disjuncture of the visual and verbal signs, Pinter moves into ecological processes. The idea of Man being in the world is what's important.

The ritual pattern of Leo's rites of passage and initiation lead him into the dominant adult culture. He arrived as the innocent novice. As the temperature (literally shown in shots of thermometers) rises, so does the tension between classes and generations, and in the border crossings of the Norfolk landscape during that hot and memorable summer. Pinter reveals at the end of the film the adult man who is out of the world, a man without passion who learned nothing about love. The intimate consciousness in relation to place has been lost. In his relationship to the natural world, through camera angles Leo is often made to look small. However, each central character is related metaphorically to the planet and its zodiac signs:

> The Archer is represented by Hugh, the ninth viscount Triming-ham, a disfigured virgin of the Boer War and ancestral owner of the hall itself. The Water Carrier, appropriately enough, is identified with the virile tenant farmer on the estate, Ted Burgess; and the family's nubile daughter, Marian, who befriends Leo as go-between in her covert amatory relationship with Ted, the younger sees as the apex of the whole structure—as the Virgin. Trimingham supplies Leo with a forging link between the boy's imaginative constructions and his social role when the viscount names him Mercury, not only the smallest planet but also the messenger of the gods. (Jones, 213)

At the end of the film, Marian and Leo have grow old. She has married out of duty, not for love. She requests from Leo one final love errand. Her son, whose father was Ted, believes that he is cursed in matters of the heart. Marian asks Leo to free her son, another exorcism, by explaining, "Our love was a beautiful thing, wasn't it? Tell him he can feel proud to be descended from our union, the child of so much happiness and beauty. Tell him—" (Pinter, 367).

The interruption of sound and the shot of the car arriving at the top of the hill is the image appearing under Marian's speech. The next shot which Pinter describes is that of Brandham Hall where now "The elms have been cut down. . . . A cloud of dust from car slightly obscures the view" (Pinter, 367). The final moment does not reveal Leo's acceptance or rejection of this final task but centers on the environment itself. It implies change, and whether this change is progress is questionable in the last moments of dust swirling around the symbol of the nineteenth-century manor.

Just before this final Pinter ambiguity, there has been a repeat of the picture's first scene of the girl in the hammock and in the background the figures dressed in white like ghosts playing croquet. In present time over this past image Marian now old speaks to the mature Leo:

> You came out of the blue to make us happy, and we made you happy, didn't we? We trusted you with our great treasure. You might never have known what it was, you might have gone through life without knowing. Isn't that so? (366)

Ironically, the camera shows us a shot of Ted slumped over. His gun is next to him. He has committed suicide. Marian goes on: "Hugh was as true as steel, he wouldn't hear a word against me" (366). Throughout the film Pinter has cut to shots of animals, and Ted's suicide has been foreshadowed as has his sexual prowess in juxtapositions of him with animals. With these cuts Pinter foregrounds the relationship of human activity with the social life among animals. For example, young Leo observes a horse auction in the village where in the distance he sees also Marian and Ted; on Ted's farm, Leo asks if horses "spoon"; he sees a mare foaling. Animal behavior is allied with that of the characters yet within the animal kingdom,

> When animals with the capacity to kill members of their own species reach a point in their battles where death would likely ensue shortly, one combatant will frequently turn aside and ferociously attack some nearby harmless object, like a tree or shrub, or in some other way inhibit his killing behavior or expend it harmlessly. "Honor" among animals is apparently often satisfied by the safe discharge of aggression as well as by its more lethal expression, and the battle will normally end with maximum face-saving and minimum of bloodletting. (Meeker, 64)

Ted kills a rabbit and peppers some rooks. Harmless beasts. These scenes predict his own death. A flock of geese, birds that mate for life, fly over. A dog named Dry Toast sleeps on the bed with Leo and his friend Marcus. Pinter presents a harmless bestiary. There is a herd of deer on the estate. They are totally appropriate for signaling the English estate. In one frame they appear to substitute for the aristocracy: a herd of gentle, use-less, but isolated and restricted group, they turn and watch Leo in the delivery of his last and fatal letter. The aggression seems left to the human race. Cricket and croquet become overt substitutions for hostile acts. The killing of love by Trimingham as he sends Ted away to war or as Lady Maudsley forces Leo to reveal Marian's secret seem much more dangerous.

Following the pattern cited by Katherine Burkman in *The Arrival of Godot*, the ritual sequence to Leo's becoming an adult climaxes in an unhappy birthday. The party waits for Marian, who never comes. Mrs. Maudsley, wearing a fool's cap, drags Leo in search of her daughter. In the script it is indicated that they move past the rhododendrons toward the outbuildings. Pinter places the deadly nightshade in their path (364). They interrupt the assignation. Discovering Marian and Ted making love, Mrs. Maudsley turns Leo's head away. Writing about Pinter's play *The Birthday Party*, Burkman says: "Pinter uses the ritual of a birthday party to crystalize the seasonal nature of the drama of the dying-and-reviving god with whom man associates the death and rebirth of vegetation (Frazer) or the death and rebirth of the world itself (Eliade)" (67).

In *The Go-Between*, with its goings between the natural world and that physical world which humans have fashioned, Pinter implies a cer-tain deadly intention in the necessary pulling up of the belladonna plant and in the annoyance of those disease-bearing flies that appear at the fatal cricket match and which buzz maliciously around the perfect Victorian picnic scene. The lushness of Michel Legrand's music, which underscores the action, reinforces a sense of freedom in Leo's flights from house to farm—on the surface that might imply a Romantic view of nature. English landscapes in the late eighteenth-century and early nineteenth-century were designed to imitate the pastoral perfection of Greek mythol-ogy. Pinter puts to use the references to myth and employs ritual motifs, yet the path that Leo must follow is that of a wild and overgrown terrain.

Still, in contrast, the interruption of nature's spontaneity into the correctness of manicured garden, plants raised tidily in greenhouses, and animals put to human use and pleasure show that the external world operates best under human control and reinforces the ideals, prestige, privilege, and position enjoyed by the upper class. The love affair is placed in an uncared for section of the estate, and Pinter's screen image suggests a past in decay. The locations tamed and untamed hint at political sub-version rather than praise for the hegemonic constructs exemplified by these natural and physical worlds.

Interestingly, the film's major ecological position is apparent in Pinter's own garden. As a site in the film of his play *Betrayal,* his own garden was used. His big house with its terrace, where an electronic device (which may be read as a form of torture) sizzles any insects that trespass, connects by a winding path and herbaceous borders to the carriage house where he often writes. Walls and fences separate the inhabitants from their neighbors. Covered in a variety of creepers and climbers, the Pinter plants are ordered while the neighbors' are chaotic. A few old large trees provide a shady spot or two. Gardening is left to the gardeners. It is a place for postprandial cocktails, for viewing nature in comfort. It suggests the superiority of Humans and civilization over the world of flora and fauna. Pinter's art and the writer himself reflect and comment on nature but remain comfortably apart from its untidiness. This attitude is clearly reflected in his screenplay for *The Go-Between.*

NOTE

1. David Caute, *Joseph Losey: A Revenge on Life* (New York: Oxford University Press, 1994), p. 254.

FIGURE 4. *The Last Tycoon.* Ingrid Boulting as Kathleen Moore and Robert De Nero as filmmaker Monroe Star. Paramount Pictures. Jerry Ohlinger Archives.

CHAPTER FOUR

⊞

The Tragedy of Illusion: Harold Pinter and The Last Tycoon

KATHERINE H. BURKMAN AND MIJEONG KIM

I have been half in love with easeful death . . .

—John Keats, "Ode to a Nightingale"

When Harold Pinter adapted F. Scott Fitzgerald's 1941 unfinished novel, *The Last Tycoon*, for a film released in 1976, some critics complained that he had missed the mark. Irene Kahn Atkins suggested that Pinter did not know Hollywood "as it was or is today" (110). Others claimed that he was too morose for Fitzgerald's kind of romance. The combination of Pinter as writer, Elia Kazan as director, and Robert De Niro as performer was considered as much of a mismatch as that of Pinter with Fitzgerald.[1] On the more positive side, Roger Greenspun liked De Niro's performance: "I think it may be a great performance," he wrote, "though at first sight it is rather plain, unassuming, and free of the feints and defenses that for some people constitute important acting." Richard Eder found the film a "decent and intelligent tribute" to Fitzgerald's "burning fragment."[2] The film, however, deserves further assessment,

55

both as a masterful adaptation of the American novel and as a significant attainment in its own right. As Pinter completed the unfinished novel in his script, in many ways he made it his own.

Pinter has chosen to foreground a scene in the novel in which Fitzgerald's protagonist, the film producer Monroe Stahr, instructs one of his writers on the art of script writing. When the British writer, George Boxley, is at a loss, Stahr advises him to give up the dueling scenes and false dialogue that he associates with Hollywood. He expands his lesson by suggesting that Boxley imagine a scene without dialogue. Pinter lifts the scene from the novel, pairing away some of the description and giving stage directions so that Stahr acts out his scenario:

> Suppose you're in your office. You've been fighting duels all day. You're exhausted.
>
> *He sits.*
>
> This is you.
>
> *He stands.*
>
> A girl comes in.
>
> *He goes to the door, opens it, comes back in, shuts it.*
>
> She doesn't see you. She takes off her gloves, opens her purse and dumps it out on the table.
>
> *He mimes these actions.*
>
> You watch her.
>
> *He sits.*
>
> This is you.
>
> *He stands.*
>
> She has two dimes, a nickel and a matchbox. She leaves the nickel on the table, puts the two dimes back into her purse, takes her gloves to the stove, opens it and puts them inside.
>
> *He mimes this while talking.*
>
> She lights a match. Suddenly the telephone rings. She picks it up.
>
> *He mimes this.*
>
> She listens. She says, "I've never owned a pair of black gloves in my life." She hangs up, kneels by the stove, lights another match. (Pinter, *The Last Tycoon*, 228–29)

As Stahr further depicts the burning of the gloves, the girl is watched, he asserts, by a man whom the woman had not noticed in the room, he captures Boxley's interest. First, Boxley wants to know what happens and then what the nickel was for. Stahr claims he doesn't know what happens: "I was just making pictures" (229), he explains. The nickel, it seems, was for the movies.

Pinter, however, has left out Boxley's response in the novel that "It's just melodrama," and Stahr's retort, "Not necessarily" (Fitzgerald, 43). Herein lies the key to the film. Fitzgerald had created a novel that many rightly predicted might have been his best had he finished it. But if one reads the plans for the chapters that were never written because of Fitzgerald's untimely death, one cannot help but see them as melodrama. The love story, which is central to the first six chapters, takes several more turns as Stahr becomes the victim of murder plots, a plane crash, and more (Fitzgerald, 162–68). Pinter's decision, however, was to use the material Fitzgerald had finished, shaping it as a tragedy, not the melodrama that it might have become. The tragedy that Pinter so adeptly perceived and completed in his film is that of illusion.

The film begins with the illusion of film itself: Monroe Stahr is making editorial suggestions about three clips from black-and-white movies. We immediately see that Stahr shapes illusion in film as a creative artist, not just a business tycoon. But *The Last Tycoon* is also about how illusion invades Stahr's life and how he confuses the world of film that he creates with the world in which he lives and cannot control—hence, his tragic fall. That fall is symbolized by *The Last Tycoon's* last moment, in which Stahr disappears into a sound stage, consumed by the black-and-white world of illusion that he had confused with his own life.

The first glimpse of Stahr's face (only his back is seen as he edits the films that introduce the picture) occurs when he is awakened by an earthquake. Since a studio guide has just given a tour and answered questions about how to give the illusion of an earthquake, and since this is a film, the boundaries between illusion and reality appear as blurred, even as Stahr seems to awake to a "real" earthquake. With the metafilmic emphasis of Pinter's script, Stahr's awakening from a world of dream is questionable from the outset, much as Deborah's awakening in the playwright's later drama, *A Kind of Alaska* would prove to be.

The confusion of dream and reality continues when Stahr sees two women float by on a dislodged, oversized head of the goddess Siva and he recognizes in one of them, Kathleen Moore, who bears a likeness to his beloved dead wife, Minna Davis. The primal illusion, it would seem, then, is that of death overcome, perhaps the primal illusion of all art. Since his wife's death, Stahr has immersed himself in shaping the illusion of film itself, all but living in the studio which he rules like a king. Significantly, however, his great love for Minna began only when she was near death: "I was closest to her . . . when she was dying" (242), he tells Kathleen. Then, too, the goddess Siva represents both the forces of salvation and destruction and, as she seems to deliver Kathleen to Stahr, her gift surely contains the seeds of death.

Indeed, death intrudes from the outset as part of the world of illusion, making itself felt as melodrama in the initial film-within-a-film in the form of a gangland killing. Later it makes a more comic appearance with the demise of a film editor during a screening while nobody notices. Jeff opines, "Eddie . . . probably didn't want to disturb the screening, Mr. Brady" [230]. But the tragic potential of death dominates as quite early in the film we also come to see that Stahr is himself a dying man. One scene reveals a doctor ministering to Stahr, a doctor whose advice he clearly is not taking:

DOCTOR: When are you taking that vacation?

STAHR: Oh, some time. Six weeks or so.

. . . .
. . . .

DOCTOR: Need any more pills?

Stahr pats his pocket.

STAHR: Fine.

DOCTOR: Any pain?

STAHR: Some. (210)

The style is understated, the situation clear. Stahr, the "boy wonder" (235), the "Vine Street Jesus" (251), whose charismatic leadership of the studio will make his fall a tragic one, is dying and is doing nothing to change the lifestyle that is, in his case, lethal. Death, portrayed in the film first as melodramatic then as comic, is finally portrayed as tragic, not just because the star/Stahr is falling but because the world that he inhabits and whose creative center he has become is also coming to an end. Like the young and dying John Keats, whose love for the beautiful song of the nightingale was interwoven with a yearning for the release of death, so for the young and dying Stahr, the world of illusion, which draws him and which he fuels, has death at its core. And, like all tragic heroes (at least the Aristotelian, classical variety), Stahr's movement is toward realization or recognition of his situation and of himself.

Fitzgerald had suggested this death in and of Hollywood theme in his novel, partly by creating Stahr as a mixture of the famous producer Irving Thalberg (considered historically to be the last of the artistic Hollywood tycoons), of himself, and of some fictional or mythical king, who like all kings, must die. Kathleen, the woman who so resembles Stahr's first wife, describes her previous lover as a real king, but adds: "He wasn't really much like a king. Not nearly as much as you" (243). Pinter scripts the film and De Niro plays the part in a manner that brings the particular crisis of Stahr's reign into the world of myth:

As Stahr, De Niro stalks the film like a variation of some mythological creature, like Icarus in executive dress. It's as if he is part man, part camera, and camera endowed with animal quickness and discriminating consciousness. He doubles as the film's energy and as its energy source. As he articulates it, energy comes to represent Hollywood's potential—a world of fluidity and endless possibilities which, and here's the rub, are played out according to the contradictions of the country. (Callahan, 208)

Those contradictions are the exterior ones represented by the New York executives who are Hollywood's investors. They are the producers and lawyers who will take over after the "last tycoon" and make Hollywood a strictly commercial venture; we see them in the film, impatient with Stahr's desire to make the occasional quality film that will lose money (Pinter, 214), indulgent with their "boy wonder," but anticipating with some pleasure his inevitable fall. Interior contradictions abound as well, however, involving Stahr's paternalistic role as king of the universe to which he gives life and which is sucking his blood.

The three antagonists with whom Stahr must deal in the studio world of the film are Brady, Boxley, and Brimmer. Pat Brady, played by Robert Mitchum, defines himself as "the strong base on which Monroe Stahr rests" (198) and is the executive who "handles" Stahr for the New York moguls who sponsor the studio. Unlike Stahr, who refuses even to have his name appear on the pictures that he produces, Brady craves recognition. His treatment of his daughter Cecilia like a prized possession and his sexual conquest of his secretary, which Cecilia unwittingly interrupts, further characterize Brady as crudely opportunistic. One senses early on that if this man is indeed the base on which the gifted Stahr rests, then Stahr is in trouble.

Stahr is also in trouble with his writers. Boxley, played by Donald Pleasance, is the writer who, despite Stahr's best efforts, can't seem to get the hang of Hollywood writing. Boxley poses a threat to Stahr, boasting of the European tradition with which the self-educated Stahr is unfamiliar, standing on the side of narrative, logic, and individuality, all inimical to Stahr's Hollywood. His method of putting several writers on a script offends Boxley, as it does Wylie White, and neither seems to have the kind of vision that has made Stahr so successful with film. While Stahr is able simply to have Boxley's work rewritten, his mixture of contempt and respect for his writers is part of what makes him vulnerable to Brimmer, played by Jack Nicholson, the Communist organizer who purports to stand up for the writers.

In an earlier scene, Brady had suggested that the writers would never be unionized because "they'd sell each other for a nickel" (211), the nickel for a film, perhaps, that we heard about as Stahr instructed Boxley about writing for film. Again, however, Stahr has a more complex attitude, although it is as paternalistic as Brady's. When Stahr finally confronts Brimmer near the film's end, he insists that he likes and understands writers: "I don't think I've got more brains than a writer. I just think his brains belong to me. I know how to use them," he asserts bluntly (267). Stahr's drunken fight with Brimmer, which follows his rejection by Kathleen, brings him down, but throughout one can see the forces waiting to pounce, the hubris that Stahr has mixed with his modesty, that makes him miscalculate his invulnerability in the studio world. The camera lingers on Brady, often flanked by the New York lawyer Fleishaker, played by Ray Milland, tracing their growing disdain for and anxiety about Stahr's highhanded methods. In an early scene, a studio guide had pointed out Stahr's office high up in a building, giving an early sense that power resides above. After Stahr's fiasco with Brimmer, though, Brady is given the role of camera, looking down at his prey from a window above, assuming the power that he will now wield against his victim (271).

Pinter has, of course, always been fascinated with the play of power, and Stahr's defeat at the hands of the various organizations, the commercial power represented by Brady, the writer/union power by Boxley and

Brimmer (Boxley seems to leave defeated, but his cause is taken up by Brimmer) is reminiscent of the defeat of such Pinter creations as Stanley in *The Birthday Party*, Spooner in *No Man's Land*, or Teddy in *The Homecoming*. The effect here, however, is far more tragic than in the case of his own less heroic characters, and in this tragedy of illusion Stahr moves to greater insight than is attained by most other Pinter protagonists.

It is partly his role as camera that defines Stahr's tragic role. When Callahan calls De Niro as Stahr "part man, part camera" (208), he touches, perhaps unwittingly, on the particular way in which Pinter has scripted his film as the tragedy of illusion. "The camera is the narrator," Callahan points out, "and there is the added touch of shooting Stahr as he would have liked to have shot himself—in motion, a personification of the moving picture" (209). Stahr as narrator/camera and object of the camera or the subject that the camera captures is also the personification of death, in the sense that Christian Metz has explored in "The Imaginary Signifier," that film can only reveal what is absent, already gone:

> In film, Metz explains, the actor is present at shooting when the audience is not, but is absent during the film's projection, leaving only a "tracing" on the screen. Thus cinema always presents us with a "double withdrawal" represented by our own distance from the screen and by the delegated image of absent-objects being traced there. (quoted in Michaels, 116)

With its constant use of metafilmic devices, Pinter's filmscript continually makes us aware of the tragic implications of Stahr's inevitable fall from grace and of the absence and death at the heart of film's illusions. While at the same time that we are invited to see the enormous energy and brilliance with which Stahr runs the studio, at every step of the way we are also invited to see that he is walking a tightrope from which he must surely fall. The films-within-a-film themselves foreshadow that fall with their emphasis first on death and then on a woman's betrayal (Michaels, 115–16). After Stahr has seen Kathleen as the image of his dead wife in the wake of the studio earthquake, he returns home and enters his bedroom only to be greeted by Minna herself in a film saying, "Darling, I've come home" (this is not in the printed filmscript but is in the film itself). The introduction of the film clip suggests that very presence of absence which again foreshadows the impossibility of a relationship with Kathleen.

Pinter also brings out the potential tragedy in Stahr's relationship with Kathleen by using silence to designate death. Death is sensed in the lack of sound that Pinter designates in their fateful meeting:

ROBINSON: What'll we do with them, chief?

Close up. Stahr, staring. No sound. (202)

After cutting to activity and shouts about saving the settings from water, the camera again focuses on Stahr: "*Stahr alone. No sound*" (203). After further activity, the camera settles on "*Kathleen standing in the water.* No sound" (203). Joanne Klein suggests that Pinter is employing a technique here that he had used in his previous *The Proust Screenplay*. Describing their meeting in the wake of the earthquake, she notes:

> Two silent shots of Stahr and one of Kathleen from his point of view interrupt the pandemonium of the rescue operations, suggesting a transcendent negation of reality by the imagination. . . . Kathleen, in fact, persists in her mysteriousness throughout their relationship, becoming almost a figment of his mental circuits. (133)

Attracted by her distance and mysteriousness, Stahr can maintain his illusion of her perfection only if she remains unattainable. Like Keats's nightingale, she will lead him quite literally out of this world.

The paternalistic way in which Stahr operates as "king" of the studio is tinged with a narcissistic quality that also foreshadows his vulnerability to outer and inner forces of destruction. For example, despite the apparent wisdom of his firing of the inept director, Red Ridingwood, and Stahr's own ability to draw a performance from Didi, an actress with whom Ridingwood cannot cope, the touch of ruthlessness with which he handles the director will come back to haunt him when he is himself fired by the equally ruthless but less creative moguls whom he has tended to disregard. Although he is apparently able to reassure the actor Rodriguez who comes to him with his personal problem of impotence, the impression is that just as Stahr shares a ruthlessness which will catch up with him in the end, so too does he share a potential impotence which will overtake him. One of the film's tragic ironies is his ability to help Rodriguez but not himself.

For, like Narcissus himself, Stahr is unable to love. Rejecting the advances of Brady's lovely young daughter, Stahr jokingly reveals the truth: "Ah. Well, I'd marry you. I'm lonely. But I'm too old and tired to undertake anything" (206). Stahr is actually quite young; when Kathleen asks him his age, he replies, "I've lost track. About thirty-five I think" (235). Stahr has quite truly lost track—he feels old and is finally not even able to "undertake" Kathleen despite his obsession with her and his desire to possess her. Complaining of her former lover, who was too possessive with her, Kathleen senses that Stahr is pursuing her as an object to be possessed as well. Again, the moment is one of foreshadowing:

> I lived with a man, for a long time. Too long. I wanted to leave but he couldn't let me go. So finally I ran away.
>
> *Pause. She smiles at him.*
>
> I must go now. I have an appointment. I didn't tell you. (239)

Kathleen's diagnosis continues to be apt. Millions of people go to films, Stahr explains to her, because he gives them what they need. "What you need" (239), she remarks, as if she can see to the heart of his narcissistic fragility.

Stahr's narcissistic role is underscored in the film by the visual use of water. He has built a dream house on the ocean to which he brings Kathleen. The beginnings of a pool for the house are seen. When he has been rejected by Kathleen, Stahr brings Cecilia out to the ocean as well. But, most significantly, when Stahr is knocked down by Brimmer, he drags himself out to the pool at Brady's house where the confrontation has taken place and gazes, dying, into the pool. When Cecilia as rejected Echo cradles him in her arms, the image fluctuates back to that of the "Vine Street Jesus," which Brady had called him, so we have part Narcissus, part Pietà before us.

Although Kathleen's behavior with Stahr appears to be half-mysterious, half-teasing, a yes when she means no, a no when she means yes, her attraction for him is clear, yet she is outraged by his high-handed behavior (251), and there is a distinct impression that she leaves him because he does not love her so much as he loves the illusion of his dead wife. And, there has already been a hint that even that love of his wife was one of illusion. Once more the film's use of film to make its points involves Stahr's impatience with the writer Wylie whom Stahr castigates for his distortion of a girl in a film on which he is working:

You've given her a secret life. She doesn't have a secret life. You've made her a melancholic. She is not a melancholic. . . . The girl stands for health, vitality, love. You've made her a whore. (216)

However, when Kathleen insists on her secret life, Stahr treats her like a whore. Tender and considerate of her in early scenes, once she reveals something of that secret life to Stahr, her plans to marry an American who has saved her, he misreads her desire to be saved from this savior by taking out his own hurt and anger on her. The scene is disturbing in its hint of sadism: "Stop walking. . . . Come back. . . . Closer. . . . Open your coat. . . . Close your eyes" (257). Kathleen, as the omitted stage directions indicate, is obedient, but Stahr has lost the moment. Though she later agrees to see him once more, she sends a telegram instead, informing him that she has been married.

Further use of film-within-the-film seals his failure. Toward the end of *The Last Tycoon*, Stahr observes a film clip reminiscent of the ending of *Casablanca*, with its choice of husband over lover. And though the song is not in Pinter's written filmscript, the film itself includes Didi singing a farewell to her lover—"You had the chance, you had the choice." Stahr does choose Kathleen, but he has missed the moment when she might have said yes. Even though he insists that Boxley's stilted dialogue at the end of the film clip be redone (another nail in his coffin with the movie executives), it is clear that the film pales next to its original:

The significance underlying the parody in relation to the overall structure of *The Last Tycoon* is twofold: first, that the delegated image on the screen is even further withdrawn into the imaginary by referring us to an "original" filmic text, *Casablanca*; and secondly, that the present representation is an entropic version of that absent text, de-energized, degraded, and closed. Stahr can intervene, as he did on the set by removing the director, to bring about the picture's completion, but he cannot by re-shooting bring it to life. (Adams, 117)

Nor can Stahr bring his dead wife to life in Kathleen.

The objections of some critics to the quality of the film clips within the film on the grounds that Irving Thalberg would have done better or that "fifty-one-year-old Tony Curtis and forty-eight-year-old Jeanne Moreau, both well overage for the 1930s romantic leads" (Adams, 301), made the *Casablanca*-style film ludicrous, miss the point. Surely the insipid nature of the film and the aged actors were purposeful on Pinter's and Kazan's part, giving, as they do, an extraordinary sense of how Stahr is trying to revive and hold on to the past.

Michaels gets at the heart of Pinter's portrayal of the tragedy of illusion with his further suggestion that *The Last Tycoon* depicts the "natural propensity to entropy" at the heart of dreams and film itself. As shaper of "our collective dreams," Stahr, who disappears at film's end into the darkness of a sound stage, "evokes the sense of absence and entropy inherent both in our theories of cinema and in our memories of the last days of the old Hollywood" (117):

> While [the final scene] is an elegiac evocation of the aesthetic dreams once realized by certain powerful movies, it also paradoxically insures its own survival through the very act of withdrawal. As the embodiment of the cinema's expressive potential, Stahr achieves in his recession into darkness what Metz calls the "lost object" status of film, infinitely desirable because always unpossessible. . . . As Kathleen has been the lost object, the distant star, of his vital illusion, so he has become the Stahr of our own. (Michaels, 117)

In the novel several more meetings between Stahr and Kathleen after her marriage to the American are projected, but Pinter has chosen to mark her telegram about her marriage as the end of the relationship and of Stahr. The protagonist's deterioration is delineated in a few final scenes in which he fights drunkenly for his diminishing power (echoes of a drunken scene of Boxley fighting for his diminishing power), is defeated in a fistfight with the Communist labor organizer, Brimmer, and is ordered to take a long vacation by the studio executives, a polite way of pushing him out.

Pinter, however, replays the earlier scene between Stahr and Boxley about "making pictures" before giving us Stahr's final disappearance into darkness. With the former scenario now played with Kathleen as the actress burning gloves and possessing the famous nickel for the movies, the tragedy of illusion takes its final, haunting form. When Kathleen sees another man in the room, she goes to him—his designation as a blond possibly indicating that he is her American husband. Stahr has been addressing the camera and she does so too at the end, the suggestion being that both are in some way unreal, absent, the subjects of illusion. Pinter later was to give this rather lethal role to the camera in his adaptation of *The Comfort of Strangers*,[3] in which photography takes on the objectifying role of the film camera in this earlier movie. Stahr's own realization that he has been the subject rather than the controller of illusion is part of the tragic structure of the film as well, so that at the same time he has fallen, he gains a kind of transcendent knowledge that mitigates the sadness of his fate. It is as if Stahr comes to understand the secret of Pinter's own art of "making pictures," which Klein describes as "cauterizing opaque images that speak all that can be told. . . . The omnipresence of impenetrability becomes his [Stahr's] final epiphany" (Klein, 136–37).

By his constant use of metafilmic elements, Pinter has also achieved a degree of distancing in the film that might well please a theorist such as Laura Mulvey. In her classical essay, "Visual Pleasure and Narrative Cinema," Mulvey discusses the way that the gaze has been handled in mainstream Hollywood films, with spectator and hero overcoming castration anxiety as the hero comes to possess the woman and the spectator identifies with that experience (21). This Hollywood tendency to present women as objects, decried by so many feminists, is demystified and critiqued in the film, Kathleen showing some of the wisdom of several of Pinter's dramatic heroines (Ruth in *The Homecoming*, Kate in *Old Times*, Emma in *Betrayal*) who successfully resist their role as object. While the script of *The Last Tycoon* depicts the glamorized, idealized Kathleen on a pedestal (well, at least on the head of Siva), makes her mysterious and possessible at the same time (after all, she suggests the seduction at Stahr's house), and equates her with the dead wife as object, in both the script and film the use of metafilmic devices also demystify Kathleen, who wants a quiet life, who refuses to be possessed, and who does not allow Stahr to treat her as an object.

Perhaps most telling is the use of black-and-white sequences within the color sequences that dominate in the film's technique and are echoed by references to black-and-white imagery in the dialogue. The foreshadowing in the opening black-and-white film clips and the comment on the choice of husband over lover in the *Casablanca*-style film clip, tend to underline the way that illusion dominates reality and overcomes it in Stahr's experience.

When Stahr first mistakes Edna for Kathleen, thinking that Kathleen was the woman with a silver belt on the head of Siva, he explains his mistake to Edna in the car: "I've been stupid. Last night I had an idea you were the exact double of someone I knew. It was dark and the light was in my eyes" (223). The search for a double involves the world of illusion that Stahr enters in a state of confusion. When Kathleen leaves Stahr for the last time, she comments on his world, and there is the impression that her exit is from the dangers of "black-and-white" illusion. "I can never get used to the way . . . night falls here," she says. "So fast. There's no twilight. Is there?" (257).

So Pinter has shaped the drama as tragedy, depicting the fall of a great man, a king/tycoon, perhaps the last of the great film tycoons of the time, as the title of the novel and screenplay indicate. Stahr's fall is partly at the hands of forces from without but partly because of tragic flaws in his own character—his inability to love, his focus on his own needs, his assumption of some of the values of the world that he attempts to rule in a paternalistic manner. As a master of poetic repetition, Pinter, however, avoiding the melodrama that Fitzgerald had planned for his fallen tycoon, returns to Stahr's script-writing lesson to Boxley, turning it into a moment of recognition for Stahr and the audience. Giving Stahr tragic dignity as Pinter addresses the camera, Pinter allows him to write, so to speak, his own exit and hence on some level to become master of his fate after all. With echoes of Samuel Beckett's Hamm in *Endgame*, who finishes his chronicle as part of his preparation for death, Monroe Stahr takes final control of illusion in this moment of tragic victory with which Pinter has endowed *The Last Tycoon*.

NOTES

1. Critics quoted in Michael Adams, "Gatsby, Tycoons, Island, and the Film Critics" in *Fitzgerald/Hemingway Annual:1978*, ed. Matthew J. Bruccoli and Richard Layman (Detroit: Gale Research, 1979), pp. 300–02.

2. Both quoted in Adams, p. 302

3. See Burkman, "Harold Pinter's Death in Venice: *The Comfort of Strangers*," in *The Pinter Review: Annual Essays 1992–1993*, ed. Frank Gillen and Steven H. Gale (Tampa: University of Tampa Press, 1993), pp. 38–45.

FIGURE 5. *The French Lieutenant's Woman.* Meryl Streep as actress Anna portraying the nineteenth-century character Sarah Woodruff on the breakwater at Lyme. United Artists Corporation. Jerry Ohlinger Archives.

⊞

CHAPTER FIVE

Harold Pinter's
The French Lieutenant's Woman:
A Masterpiece of Cinematic Adaptation

STEVEN H. GALE

There may be some disagreement about which of Harold Pinter's sources for his cinematic adaptions is the best, but there can be no doubt that *The French Lieutenant's Woman* is his best screenplay. In watching the other films made from his scripts, viewers are often interested, involved, and appreciative that the movie is a good one. In watching *The French Lieutenant's Woman* (1981), they are fascinated from the very beginning of the picture and aware that it is an extremely good film verging on greatness. It is also the screenwriter's most inventive and imaginative screenplay. Indeed, it is the exemplar of Pinter's own declaration that with screenplays, "I don't just transcribe the novel; otherwise you might as well do the novel. In other words, these are acts of the imagination on my part!" (Gussow, 100). As Roger Ebert says, the script is "both simple and brilliant" (237), and both the film and the screenplay were nominated for Academy Awards.

John Fowles, whose 1969 novel of the same name served as Pinter's source, had been "less than happy" with two previous movies made from his novels and had spent eight or nine years trying to find the right direc-

tor to turn *The French Lieutenant's Woman* into a film. After Fred Zinne-
mann failed in a "most serious attempt" (Fowles, "Foreword," vi), Fowles
resolved to insist on veto power over the choice of director. In 1969, while
the book was still in proofs, the novelist and his agent, Tom Maschler,
decided to approach Karel Reisz about tackling the project. Reisz, having
recently finished a difficult period piece (*Isadora*), could not be tempted.
Robert Bolt also declined, on the basis that the novel was unfilmable. At
this point Fowles and Maschler determined that they needed to look for
a "demon barber . . . someone sufficiently skilled and independent to be
able to rethink and recast the thing form the bottom up" (viii); they also
decided that Pinter was "the best man for that difficult task." By happen-
stance, a development deal was offered to Fowles which included Pinter,
but the novelist was not interested in the others involved in the proposed
project. Then, in 1978, Maschler went back to Reisz, who agreed to
agree—with the proviso that Pinter had to write the script. On May 27,
1980, shooting began.

Fowles's novel is extremely popular and highly acclaimed,[1] but the
very factors that make it popular presented Pinter with an artistic challenge: how to capture the twentieth-century perspective from which the
Victorian story is told, primarily through the vehicle of numerous autho-
rial intrusions (footnotes, references, poetry quotations, opinions,
philosophies, facts, descriptions) which flavor the novel. The alternating
plotlines in the novel have a natural cinematic equivalent in parallel editing, but it is not the essentials of plotting that preoccupied the screenwriter. In an interview with Mel Gussow shortly after he finished the
script, Pinter commented, "*The French Lieutenant's Woman.* That's been
bloody, bloody hard. It's a remarkable book. The problems involved in
transposing it to film are quite considerable. It pretends to be a Victorian
novel, but it isn't. It's a modern novel, and it's made clear by the author
that he's writing it now. The whole idea had to be retained" (Gussow, 53).

Although he has used a voice-over narrator in other films, the obvi-
ous choice for retaining the Fowles touch, Pinter is on record as not being
fond of the device, and he wanted to avoid it here, if possible. Another
approach to "visualizing" the "stereoscopic vision" of the novel would be
to create a persona who is both the author and a character in the Victorian story, a device used by Max Ophuls in *La Ronde*, but Fowles did not
favor the technique (and he thought that only Peter Ustinov, with whom
he had discussed the possibility, could have managed the role). The dual
ending of the novel must have been troublesome as well. The first ending

occurs in chapter 44 with a short narration of how Charles contritely accepted a loveless marriage, which he was doomed to suffer through for the rest of his life in silent accord with Victorian tradition. In the second ending (which occurs in chapter 61, over 130 pages later), Sarah leaves. After years of searching for her, Charles, who has ended his relationship with Ernstina, finds Sarah, only to be rejected and left to rebuild his life existentially without her (or so the narrator suggests with his semi-hopeful references to a move to America and images of the sea—life goes on). Too, there was the normal dilemma of how to cut a novel-length story to fit within a typical film-length time limit (two hours and twenty-four minutes in this case), though this latter was a problem which the screenwriter had solved quite successfully in his earlier adaptations.

To begin, in Printer's script there has been an enormous amount of compression. The script is equivalent to no more than about one-sixth of the length of the novel. Indeed, Pinter cut more from his source in this adaptation than in any of his others, with the exception of *The Proust Screenplay*. The entire Winsyatt inheritance subplot is eliminated, as is most of the Sam/Mary subplot (which in some ways is equivalent to the standard eighteenth-century comedy witty couple/dull couple subplot), Mrs. Fairley's role is reduced substantially, Sam's treacherous and self-serving nondelivery of Charles's note to Sarah, which results in her leaving and Charles breaking off the engagement with Ernstina, is removed, and the Charles-and-prostitute/mother episode is left undeveloped, just to mention the major deletions. Like the rehearsal of Charles's American travels, most of the removals have little or no effect on the story line or the expression of the meaning of the novel—all that the cut material does is reveal a bit about Charles's nature and the Victorian world; it does not provide any elaboration on the theme.

There are, of course, additions and alterations. These range from Pinter's giving a name to the German doctor simply referred to in the novel as a specialist in the kind of mental problems that Dr. Grogan assumes afflict Sarah (Pinter, *The French Lieutenant's Woman*, 40; Fowles, 164) to focusing on Sarah's habit of drawing and her sketches (not dealt with in the novel but a plot device in the film) to providing a happy ending to the Victorian tale.

The addition of the name of Dr. Hartmann merely may be part of Pinter's penchant for using small details to make things appear more realistic, to touch the world outside the film that he spoke about in connection with his script for *The Caretaker*.[2] The focus on Sarah's art is more important since it prepares for her decision to move into the Elliott household as a nanny, for the early shots of her sketching establishes her desire and talent for art, which will be accommodated as one of the conditions of her employment. The close-ups of the early drawings are also used to emphasize Sarah's state of mind; she is in anguish, and the expression on the face on the self-portraits is appropriately similar to that in Edvard Munch's most famous painting, *The Scream.*

Changing the home in which Sarah takes refuge from that of Dante Gabriel Rossetti, the Pre-Raphaelite poet and painter, to that of an architect named Elliott whose gender-shifted son, Tom (perhaps with a bow to one of Pinter's favorite poets, T. S. Eliot), does several things. For one, the coincidence of her ending up at the home of one of the century's better-known and more liberal characters is a little far-fetched and maybe a bit of overkill, so an architect's abode is more realistic. For another, the introduction of Rossetti's name is a tad distracting because it captures the audience's attention and threatens to shift the focus to the poet as opposed to Fowles's story; the more anonymous name in the film version keeps the focus on the story. Still, Tom Elliott also has interesting reverberations, since Eliot was a transitional figure in the movement from Victorian to modern English literature; nevertheless, the name is common enough not to be overly diversionary. Predictably, some scenes were combined and some changes were made for purely cinematic reasons, as when action is interjected effortlessly into the discussion between Charles and Mr. Freeman, Ernstina's father, by a move in locale, exchanging the static setting of the businessman's office for a walk on the wharf (Pinter, *The French Lieutenant's Woman,* 11). Finally, Pinter's invention of a happy ending (102), the third ending to the nineteenth-century plot, is certainly more in keeping with popular Victorian models than either of the two conclusions that Fowles supplies. It is also an indispensable ingredient for expressing what the screenwriter is really writing about.

In a note prefacing the published version of his script, Pinter says, "The writing of this screenplay took over a year. This is the final version with which we began shooting. Inevitably, a number of scenes were cut and some structural changes were made during the course of production" (ii). There are a great number of differences between the script and the released film. Besides the minor word changes probably introduced by the actors during the filming, there are whole scenes that have been cut, but most of these alterations are insignificant and do not have any effect on either Fowles's or Pinter's themes.

However, this comment of Pinter's is significant because it reveals the writer's sense of pride in his work. If it were simply a matter of publishing the script, he could have published a version taken directly from the film. The added touch of stating that it took him a year to write the screenplay, when he only infrequently comments publicly on the time that it takes him to write something, reenforces the importance that he attaches to the version of the screenplay which he considers his. It may be that he feels that once the script is tinkered with by others it becomes collaborative to the point that it is not his product any more or that such tinkering for practical purposes removes some of the artistic element; he has evidenced his dissatisfaction with this kind of alteration in connection with several of his film scripts.[3] Whatever the case, it appears that he wanted to preserve what he considers the best version.

Fowles, too, has indicated his disdain for the commercial nature of film making: "in a later novel, *Daniel Martin*, I did not hide the contempt I feel for many aspects of the commercial cinema—or more exactly, since cost of production and mode of recoupment make all cinema more or less commercial, of the cinema where accountants reign, where profit comes first and everything else a long way after" ("foreword," xiii). This film also proves to some extent to be an example of such a "vile ethos," of the impact of financial considerations on the cinematic art. This is evidenced by materials in Box 18 in the Pinter Archives at the British Library in London. In an "Anna, the actress who plays Sarah" version of the script, there are seven sets of production suggestions typed on pink paper titled "*FRENCH LIEUTENANT'S WOMAN—SAVINGS*." Page 1 contains a list of pages, scenes, what has been cut, and the shooting time saved. The following are samples of the contents:

Pages	Scene		Time Saved
36	60–61	Set of INT	1/3 day
	DAIRY and Scene 60		
	OMITTED.		

SAVING SUMMARY

Sets Omitted: STUDIO

BROTHER/EXHIBITION

MRS. TRANTOR'S GARDEN ROOM

MRS. TRANTOR'S BEDROOM

MRS. TRANTOR'S PANTRY
LANDING & STAIRS
CHARLES' LONDON LIVING ROOM
CHARLES' LONDON BEDROOM
HOTEL INTERIOR—EXT
LOCATION: DAIRY INTERIOR

Days saved from previous schedule: *4 ¹/₃ days and bits.*

Additional material in Box 20 is further evidence of the economic side of the project, which extends well beyond the filming.[4] The studio heads must have been pleased to report a domestic gross of $22 million.

Undoubtedly, the primary element of which Pinter can be proud is his creation of a *coup de cinéma* by replacing the narrator with a twentieth-century story line and developing a film-within-a-film structure. What is interesting about the film version of *The French Lieutenant's Woman* is not the compression, cuts, or alterations of the source material; what is interesting is what was added, not in the normal minutiae of details or dialogue but in the concept. Even though Pinter has admitted that the idea originated with Reisz, it was the screenwriter who was responsible for the full realization of the concept.[5] The boldness and imaginativeness of this invention and its application brought an appreciative acknowledgment from Fowles:

> I am convinced now, in retrospect, that the only feasible answer was the one that Harold and Karel hit upon. We had all before been made blind to its existence by the more immediate problem of compressing an already dense and probably over-plotted book into two hours' screen time. The idea of adding an entirely new dimension and relationship to it would never have occurred to us; and quite reasonably so, with almost anyone but Harold Pinter. ("Foreword," xi)

Pinter deserves Fowles's approbation, for he captures the essentials of the novelist's Victorian story, character, and era (which is all that many readers wanted when they went to the movie), but through the utilization of the film-within-a-film construction he forefronts both the dual perspective and the underlying themes effectively.[6]

The paralleling of the two affairs as indicative of their respective societies serves to reflect the limitations of each society, the constraint of the Victorian and the license of the modern, and the film-with-a-film technique is a perfect device to demonstrate this theme by juxtaposition. For instance, the proleptic technique—Mike and Anna sleeping together foreshadows what will happen when Charles and Sarah sleep together—is introduced easily and naturally in this format.

Audience interest in and familiarity with the art of filmmaking is evident in the popularity of movie studio shorts that were run between feature presentation in the 1940s and current television specials about filmmaking, fan magazines, and Disney's MGM Studios and Universal Studios with their "backstage" tours. This a priori interest and knowledge certainly lend to the general appeal of *The French Lieutenant's Woman*.[7] And, for a contemporary audience, film provides a readily understood referential language to be use in exploring complicated abstract concepts.

Though certainly only tenuously related, there is a cinematic link with *A Double Life*, directed by George Cukor from a script by Garson Kanin, which brought Ronald Colman the 1947 Academy Award. In the movie, Colman plays a Shakespearean actor whose real life becomes intermixed with his portrayal of Othello. Ironically, this leads to his on-stage stragulation of his wife, whom he mistakenly believes guilty of Desdamona's purported sin. The sequence in which Charles, in a horse-drawn cab, tries to find Sarah in a seedy part of town is quite similar to a sequence in John Huston's *Moulin Rouge* in which José Ferrer as Henri de Toulouse-Lautrec searches for his red-haired prostitute/lover who has left him. Huston's film was released in 1952, seventeen years before Fowles's novel was published and twenty-nine years before Pinter's film adaptation, making the scene in the novel and later movie pictorially derivative, an homage, or a literary allusion used to comment upon the depth of the absolute self-degradation to which desperation drives these scorned men in their quests for their loves.

Those components of Fowles's themes that probably attracted Pinter to this project were the manipulation of time and the exploration of the nature of reality (to some extent as related to art), which throughout his career has occupied his attention in his own writing—dramas such as *The Lover, The Collection, The Homecoming, Landscape, Night, Silence, Old Times,* and *No Man's Land*—and virtually all of his film scripts up to that time. In the script the screenwriter's interests are reflected in structure and theme alike. The challenge of the adaptation must have been irresistible.

The device of a cast party at the film, which is used to bring together the characters and themes, is reminiscent of the celebratory conclusion of Lindsay Anderson's *O Lucky Man!* (1973). Perhaps surprisingly, given how dark many of Pinter's plays seem on the surface, in much of his dramatic writing, especially the major works, there is an underlying positivism and optimism. So is it with his film scripts. *The French Lieutenant's Woman* is an example of this quality. True, at the end Mike is lost in a world between reality and illusion, which he cannot distinguish between, but Anna escapes into reality, divorced from her role playing, healthy and happy in the world of her real marriage and life outside the film.

This also proves another refutation to those feminist critics who short-sightedly label Pinter a misogynist. As Michael Billington points out, Pinter takes an almost feminist line by contrasting "Anna's growing identification with Sarah, [*sic*] with Mike's concern with the purely theatrical aspects of performance" (p. 273). This feminist orientation is also evident in the figures about prostitutes that Anna reads aloud to Mike in the hotel room—figures which Pinter researched and added. The Pinter Archives Box 17 contains the note:

Ch. 2

S 1,155,000 females

7,600,000 males

−1851.

This is the referent for the following exchange which occurs in the film script:

ANNA (*referring to the book*): Listen to this. "In 1857 the Lancet estimated that there were eighty thousand prostitutes in the county of London. Out of every sixty houses one was a brothel."

MIKE: Mmm.

Pause.

ANNA (*reading*): "We reach the surprising conclusion that at a time when the male population of London of all ages was one and a quarter million, the prostitutes were receiving clients at a rate of two million per week."

MIKE: Two million!

ANNA: You know when I say—in the graveyard scene—about going to London?

Wait.

She picks up her script of The French Lieutenant's Woman, *flips the pages, finds the page. She reads aloud:*

"If I went to London I know what I should become. I should become what some already call me in Lyme."

MIKE: Yes?

ANNA: Well, that's what she's really faced with.

She picks up the book.

This man says that hundreds of the prostitutes were nice girls like governesses who had lost their jobs. See what I mean? You offend your boss, you lose your job. That's it!

You're on the streets. I mean, it's real.

Mike has picked up a calculator and starts tapping out figures.

MIKE: The male population was a million and a quarter but the prostitutes had two million clients a week?

ANNA: Yes. That's what he says.

MIKE: Allow about a third off for boys and old men. . . . That means that outside marriage—a Victorian gentleman had about two point four fucks a week.

She looks at him. (18–19)

Anna's growing identification with Sarah's character is neatly balanced by Mike's disinterested concern with numerical figures in this exchange. The irony, naturally, is that, as already indicated, in the end Anna will be able to completely distance herself from her screen persona while Mike will be totally absorbed in his.

The potential blending of the characters is seen in the script:

73. Interior. Caravan. Present. Day.

Anna in her caravan. A knock on the door.

ANNA: Hello!

Mike comes in.

MIKE: May I introduce myself?

ANNA: I know who you are.

They smile. He closes the door.

MIKE: So you prefer to walk alone?

ANNA: Me? Not me. Her.

MIKE: I enjoyed that.

ANNA: What?

MIKE: Our exchange. Out there.

ANNA: Did you? I never know. . . .

MIKE: Know what?

ANNA: Whether it's any good.

MIKE: Listen. Do you find me—?

ANNA: What?

ANNA: What?

MIKE: Sympathetic.

ANNA: Mmm. Definitely.

MIKE: I don't mean me. I mean him.

ANNA: Definitely.

MIKE: But you still prefer to walk alone?

ANNA: Who? Me—or her?

MIKE: Her. You like company.

> *He strokes the back of her neck.*

Don't you?

ANNA (*smiling*): Not always. Sometimes I prefer to walk alone.

MIKE: Tell me, when you said that—outside—you swished your skirt—very provocative. Did you mean it?

ANNA: Well, it worked. Didn't it?

> *Third Assistant's face at door.*

THIRD ASSISTANT: We're going on. (25–26)

The actors have difficulty keeping straight which "me" and "you" they are talking about, and the intrusion of the Third Assistant is an abrupt reminder to the audience that there is a third reality (an idea reenforced by the character's title), that which the audience itself belongs to, which is entirely off-screen, even though as viewers in suspended disbelief they may have been caught up temporarily in the duality being experienced by the on-screen characters.

An even more arresting example of Pinter's understanding of cinematic technique and his talent to use that knowledge effectively follows. It is a masterful scene created by Pinter that demonstrates how easily the fictional and the real sets of lives can become conjoined:

78. Interior. Hotel. Empty billiard room. Night. Present.

Mike and Anna rehearsing, holding scripts.

MIKE: Miss Woodruff!

ANNA: Just a minute, I've lost the place.

She turns pages of script.

MIKE: I suddenly see you. You've got your coat caught in brambles. I see you, then you see me. We look at each other, then I say: "Miss Woodruff."

ANNA: All right.

MIKE: Right. I see you. Get your coat caught in the bramble.

She mimes her coat caught in bramble.

MIKE: Right. Now I'm looking at you. You see me. Look at me.

ANNA: I am.

MIKE: Miss Woodruff!

ANNA: I'm looking at you.

MIKE: Yes, but now you come towards me, to pass me. It's a narrow path, muddy.

She walks toward him.

You slip in the mud.

ANNA: Whoops!

She falls.

MIKE: Beautiful. Now I have to help you up.

ANNA: Let's start over again.

She goes back to the chair.

I've got my coat caught in the brambles. Suddenly you see me. Then
I see you.

MIKE: Miss Woodruff!

*She mimes her coat caught in brambles, tugs at it walks along car-
pet towards him. He steps aside. She moves swiftly to pass him, and
slips. She falls to her knees. He bends to help her up. She looks up
at him. He stops for a moment, looking down, and then gently lifts
her. With his hand on her elbow, he leads her towards the window.*

I dread to think, Miss Woodruff, what would happen if you should
one day turn your ankle in a place like this.

She is silent, looking down.

He looks down at her face, her mouth.

ANNA: I must . . . go back.

MIKE: Will you permit me to say something first? I know I am a
stranger to you, but—

Sharp cut to:

79. Sarah turning sharply. A branch snapping. (30–31)

In the film, the called-for jump cut takes place as Anna moves to
pass Mike and she slips. The slip becomes a magnificently seamless slide
into the Victorian story, a transition that carries the action immediately
into the next sequence and the modern couple has become the Victori-
ans. It is a beautifully efficacious cut used to weld the past and the present, the real and the imagined, together. The kicker here, of course, is
that even the "real" lives are only reel lives on a silver screen.

While the differences between Pinter's published film script for *The
French Lieutenant's Woman* and the film itself are extremely complicated
and interesting, they are of a nature consonant with those explored above
in relation to many of his other screenplays. Scenes 73 and 78 in the published version, for instance, simply are brought closer together in the
movie and thus more clearly reenforce one another with the deleting of
several intervening short scenes. Still, a quick glance at the archival material reveals how hard the screenwriter labors to achieve a desired effect,
that his achievements are not accidental.

For instance, in the archival materials there are two interrelated categories of changes that Pinter makes which show a meticulous attention

to details, the striving to get things just right.[8] These include alterations in the opening sequence and the closing sequence.

On November 24, 1978, the first shot was described thus:

Clapper Board

FLW

Shooting toward shore.

Pan with figure of a woman, eventually revealing that she stands at end of stone pier staring out to sea.

On November 29, the shot becomes:

EXT. THE COBB DAY.

A clipboard. On it is written FLW Shot 1, Take 3. It shuts and withdraws. Revealed is the Cobb, a stone pier in the harbours of Lynne. The camera is shooting towards the shore. It pans with the figure of a woman, moving towards the end of the Cobb. She reaches the end and stands still, staring out to sea.

By May 1, 1979 the opening scene had been altered to read:

It shuts and withdraws, leaving a close shot of Sarah. The actress is holding her hair in place against the wind.

VOICE (*off*): All right. Let's go.

About a month and a half later (June 17), the fourth draft includes: "It shuts and withdraws, leaving a close shot of Sarah," and the time of day is dawn. The establishing time was day, but it was changed to dawn and back to day in the third draft. In a June 28 version, the slug line is:

1. ext. cobb. lyme regis. dawn. 1867.

The published wording is identical to that of the June 28 version. Finally, a tan folder containing fifty-one pages of "RETYPES FROM FINAL VERSION" ("Final" meaning the version to be submitted), changes designated by the use of red ink, includes the handwritten notation, "Anna, the actress who plays Sarah."

The published version is:

1. Exterior. The Cobb. Lyme Regis. Dawn. 1967.

A clipboard. On it is written: THE FRENCH LIEUTENANT'S WOMAN. *SCENE 1. TAKE 3.*

It shuts and withdraws, leaving a close shot of Anna, the actress who plays Sarah. She is holding her hair in place against the wind.

VOICE (*off screen*): All right. Let's go.[9]

The actress nods, releases her hair. The wind catches it.

Among other things, Pinter is trying to capture and unobtrusively draw the attention to the duality of the Sarah/Anna character.

The changes in the ending are more intriguing. The first version is in Box 17. The setting is "EXT. HOUSE. NIGHT" (p. 164, Sc. 227 in the script). Mike calls out "Anna?" which becomes "Anna!" Then there is a holograph addition:

> *M runs across courtyard, up grass slope as the Merc*
> *(Mercedes)* ~~passes~~ *goes out of gate. He cries out.*
> *M–Anna!*
> *Piano music begins.*
> *T.O.*[10]

A different version appears in Box 19:

> *New 243. ext. house*
> *Anna's white car driving towards the gate.*
> *New 244. ext. house. window.*
>   *Mike at window. He calls out:*
> MIKE: Sarah!

The published screenplay is the same as the Box 19 version. In the film's happy ending, the rowboat with Charles and Sarah in it is seen entering the lake again.

Intriguingly, Box 20 contains yet another version:

~~228~~ *240. dissolve into int. house. studio*

LONG SHOT. DAY.

*In the background the piano playing. Sunlight falls across the
room through the long windows.*

Charles and Sarah stand, embracing.

The camera tracks towards them and stops.

They kiss.

CHARLES (*softly*): Sarah.

The choices between these alternate endings is crucial. Pinter
wanted to follow Fowles's lead with multiple endings and the possibilities
that they engender, but the differences between each of those that the sce-
narist considered creates a unique meaning for his work. If Mike calls
after Anna, as in the first instance, the movie is merely the story to two
actors who have an affair, one of whom cannot admit that it has ended.
If the tale ends with Charles and Sarah together in the studio, we are back
in the Victorian story, and the film no longer seems to have anything but
a fictive grounding; the sense of any off-screen applicability is lost. Philo-
sophically, the ending that Pinter chose is the most challenging, and it fits
the thematic structure of the novel and film alike. The tacking on of a
repeat of the happy ending rowboat scene in the film itself draws the audience back into the Victorian story, yet it adds a sense of romantic unreal-
ism to it rather than being too pat like the studio ending. This dream-like
event mirrors Mike's sensitivity at the film's conclusion, for even though
he has lost Anna/Sarah, it is likely that he will live in a continuing fantasy
instead of coping with reality, an ending foretold in Pinter's stage play *The
Lover.*

Obviously, the screenwriter fine-tuned his material constantly and
over a considerable amount of time in order to get what he considered the
exact word or right combination or order of scenes. Sometimes he went
back and forth between options several times before deciding on the final
version. Just as obviously, it is not an accident that Pinter arrived successfully at the one approach which would accommodate all of the points of
the Fowles novel cinematically—the introduction of this new element in
the form of a modern framework within and through which the film-

within-a-film retains the essence of Fowles's masterpiece—and at the same time makes the screenplay of *The French Lieutenant's Woman* a masterpiece in its own right.

NOTES

1. Among other things, it was a Book-of-the Month Club selection, and between 1970 and 1981, the Signet paperback edition went through twenty-seven printings. The cover of the paperback edition that followed the Paralon Production/United Artists release of the film showed how some American publishers take liberties with everything: there is a picture of Meryl Streep as Sarah in the opening sequence when she is on the stone breakwater wearing her hooded cloak, looking back; there is also an artist's rendering of the two standing on the breakwater and kissing, an improbable invention by the book's cover artist.

2. Pinter's reference (and Fowles's "clever German doctor") is probably to Eduard von Hartmann, a metaphysical philosopher who wrote about the melancholy career of the unconscious. Hartmann's best-known work was *Die Philosophie des Unbewussten* (*The Philosophy of the Unconscious*), published in 1870. Although the time of the film is identified as 1867, and Pinter is very careful about historical facts, the period is the same and it is likely that someone like Dr. Grogan could have read some of Hartmann's papers before the three-volume was published. That Pinter would know—or, more likely, find out—such a detail speaks to the seriousness with which he approaches his art.

3. Most notably *The Handmaid's Tale*, which he considered so much altered that he has refused to allow the script to be published, and *The Remains of the Day*, which he refused to allow his name to be attached to for the same reason (see Edward T. Jones's "On *The Remains of the Day:* Harold Pinter Remaindered," in this volume).

4. Included are two letters and a release form for the video cassette of *The French Lieutenant's Woman* (for Pinter, on VHS), dated January 6, 1983, from Pat Kinsman (Pinter's secretary) to Bill Hughes, United Artists London, and December 23, 1982, to Leon from Hughes regarding the cassette. The release form (signed by Pinter) is dated 21 December 1982. A paper-clipped set of papers titled "Correspondence" includes:

> Page proofs for the Little, Brown edition of the script (photocopy with proofreading marks).

> October 29, 1980: Tom Maschler (Jonathan Cape, London) to Pinter, "When may I expect the script?"

November 4, 1980: Pinter to Maschler—script gone to Nick Hern.

December 15, 1980: Pinter to Fowles, agreeing on the Little, Brown/NAL publishing deal.

March 4, 1981: Pinter to Fowles concerning Reisz's desire to cut the last scene between Charles and Grogan.

May 13, 1981: enclosing colophon sheets, author's questionnaire, photograph for back jacket, proof of jacket (photograph and proof in file).

May 15, 1981: to Ray Roberts (senior editor at Little, Brown); two photographs of Pinter for back jacket.

June 1, 1981: from Kinsman to Roberts, a signed colophon sheet sent to Fowles's agent; enclosed is a list of works, major awards, honorary doctorates; photograph of Reisz, Fowles, and Pinter approved for the back jacket of the book.

September 11, 1981: to Pinter from Roberts, six copies of the book.

October 5, 1981: to Pinter from Roberts, enclosing a signed edition of *The French Lieutenant's Woman* screenplay and the news that there are "orders for over 500 copies of this signed edition, so it has already sold out. The film seems to be a great hit; both theatres have long lines for every show."

November 23, 1981: to Pinter from Roberts regarding reviews of the film (especially one by Vincent Canby in the *New York Times*) and noting that the movie is still in three theatres in Manhattan, with "long lines down the blocks for each show."

November 24, 1981: Pinter to Maschler.

December 10, 1981: to Pinter from Roberts, who sends along "a specially bound edition" of *The French Lieutenant's Woman* with the observation that the "film continues to do well."

5. Michael Billington, *The Life and Work of Harold Pinter* (London: Faber and Faber, 1996), p. 272.

6. Unfortunately, for those familiar with the film only in the commercial television version, the reaction may be one of confusion. Thirty minutes of "extraneous" material was omitted, to the detriment of plot, structure, and theme.

7. Besides Pinter's own *The Last Tycoon*, there are numerous films in which filmmaking is a subject, Federico Fellini's *8½* and Francois Truffaut's *Day for Night* being among the most famous.

8. He even composed a list of the names of selected authors of the epigraphs that appeared in the novel: Chapter 9, Matthew Arnold; Chapter 17,

Thomas Hardy; Chapter 35, Charles Darwin; Chapter 41, Alfred Lord Tennyson; Chapter 55, Lewis Carroll; and so on.

9. In the film, the words are, "OK. You ready, Anna?"

10. T.O. stands for titles over.

FIGURE 6. *The Comfort of Strangers*. Natasha Richardson as Mary and Rupert Everett as her lover Colin. Skouras Pictures. Jerry Ohlinger Archives.

CHAPTER SIX

⊞

Daddy Dearest:
Harold Pinter's
The Comfort of Strangers

ANN C. HALL

Harold Pinter's success as a screenwriter is nowhere more apparent than in the brilliant film, *The Comfort of Strangers* (1991), based upon the Ian McEwan novel of the same name (1981). Many critics agree that Pinter's screenplay is not merely an adaptation of the novel, but that it creates another, perhaps more powerful, work of art (Hudgins, 54; Rafferty, 82; Wilmington, F13). Katherine Burkman takes these observations one step further, arguing that as a screenplay writer Pinter perhaps occupies the unusual position of having influenced the very novel that he adapts (38).

One of the most noticeable differences between the novel and the screenplay is Pinter's focus on visual elements: the conscious references to camera work, photography, and the very nature of spectacle, watching and being watched—precisely the elements necessary to transform the novel into a film. By focusing on the spectacular, Pinter not only heightens "the sense of an ominous threat to" the British couple (Hudgins, 54), he also magnifies the relationship between spectacle and oppression and calls the entire mechanism of moviemaking into question. Truly, "we are invited to see ourselves seeing" in this screenplay (Burkman, 43), but we are also forced to see that our status as viewers is far from detached. In this screenplay, speculation is inherently ambiguous. Situations are not what they seem, and when we participate in speculation, we are also engaged in power relationships, frequently characterized in terms of the oppression of the object viewed by the subject viewing. Given this, the audience can either merely dismiss the screenplay's action as deviant or trust what they see.

As is true with all tourists, the British couple, Colin and Mary, enter a new environment to see sights, as well as to revive their failing relationship. Both the novelist and the screenwriter go to great lengths to depict the mysterious nature of their holiday locale. McEwan's decision to leave the city's name unspecified heightens the readers' sense of disorientation. The travelers themselves are so disoriented that they need maps, some the size of tables, in order to navigate through the city (McEwan, 19). Even gender distinctions are blurred in this shadowy foreign world: "It was possible to buy cigarettes here and not know whether it was a man or woman who sold them" (20).

Initially, Pinter's screenplay seems to be more straightforward. He identifies the holiday city as Venice, and we are presented with images that clearly depict the camera as our map to the city, a mechanism that appears to offer the truth of Venice by being able to go places and see things that the tourists cannot. The film opens with the camera deftly probing the home of the enigmatic Robert who will later befriend and subsequently betray the couple. Here, the camera-as-camera appears to have both wide-angle and close-up access to all of the contents of the apartment, a position that implies the camera's superior ability to ferret out truth.

In the film, director Paul Schrader chooses to linger briefly upon a large bed in a master bedroom, an image that does not appear in either the novel or the screenplay. The sequence is reminiscent of Lawrence Olivier's 1936 version of *Hamlet* which also presents the camera penetrating the Danish castle, probing its outer walls to reveal a massive bed. The allusion to this particular play is telling because in *Hamlet*, as in *Comfort*, things are not always as they seem.

As if to underscore this point, the screenplay highlights the artistic elements of the apartment, showing us artworks, lovely furniture, the beauty of Venice—the very reasons that people travel to this Italian metropolis. The Andro Badalamenti score lulls viewers further into the luxury of the spectacle. Almost immediately, however, several ambiguous images appear: a sideboard boasts brass knobs in the shape of women's heads, and "on top of the sideboard a tray of silver-backed men's hair and clothes brushes, a decorated china shaving bowl, several cut-throat razors arranged in a fan" (3). In the novel, McEwan does not present these supplies until later in the novel and without such rich detail. Here, in this early stage of the screenplay, they foreshadow the brutal events that will occur by the end of the film, as well as, importantly, offering us some insight into the violent underside of the beauty of Venice and perhaps culture in general. Symbols of art, sexuality, luxury, and civilization are literally undercut by the men's razors "arranged in a fan." McEwan's narrative constructs confusion, while Pinter's screenplay capitalizes on the camera to show, ironically, that there is more to this world than meets the eye. Despite the ambiguity of images, beauty and violence, the camera still appears to offer great insights into the Venetian world.

As the camera moves throughout this opening scene, Robert's voice is heard beginning the story that he will reiterate throughout the screenplay, the tale of his father, sisters, and wife. In the McEwan novel, Robert only tells the story once, so Pinter's decision to focus on this speech throughout the film is a significant one. Here, the voice coincides with the camera and, combined with the other masculine imagery in this opening scene, it is clear that we are entering a male world. The very first words that we hear in the film are, "My father was a very big man" (3). And, as Robert tells Colin and Mary later, it would be impossible for him to tell him about his wife "without describing my mother and sisters. And that would only make sense if I first described my father" (15).

The supremacy of the father in Robert's world and the supremacy of Robert's story in the Pinter screenplay offer a compelling and disturbing representation of patriarchy, but one that is consistent with feminist thought and closely tied to narrative structure. For many feminists such as Virginia Woolf ("A Room of One's Own"), Laura Mulvey, and Elaine Showalter, male-dominated narratives not only reflect patriarchal culture, they create, infuse, and defend all aspects of society. Luce Irigaray argues similarly, showing that the focus on the father as the originator of life, desire, and narrative, typifies patriarchy and patriarchal relationships. And, she characterizes these relationships as "homosocial." That is, patriarchy is based upon homosocial relationships, men relating to men either competitively or loyally and familially. Even in heterosexual relations, the overriding impulse is homosocial. Women are merely incidental, as decorative as the brass handles on the sideboard that Pinter takes pains to point out. While Pinter may or may not be conscious of these allusions, it is clear from his opening that Robert represents a patriarchal understanding of the world, and his privileged position as speaker and even guide through this unusual world indicates that he and men like him control this spectacle.

Colin and Mary, on the other hand, are blinded by the city's mysteries and adrift emotionally. Their relationship is in shambles, and they hope the holiday will offer some solutions. In the novel, McEwan depicts their problems by describing their lack of communication, their literal brooding silence. Not surprisingly, in Pinter's screenplay how the couple do not communicate is demonstrated through their conversations, a technique that many think defines Pinter's style.[1] When we first meet the couple in the screenplay, for example, Colin petulantly complains about the manuscript that he must read during his vacation, while Mary tries to telephone her children in England. While Colin sulks on the bed, Mary literally "connects" with the children. Subsequent scenes function similarly, with the couple talking and jibing at one another but avoiding significant discussion about their relationship and its problems.

It is no surprise, then, that the couple gravitates towards Robert, a man who appears to be in control of his destiny, and who possesses a personal narrative, albeit strange. His prowess is reflected in his ability to navigate the streets of Venice. In a number of shots with sinister overtones, Pinter depicts Robert appearing almost out of thin air and disappearing into crowds like a Venetian god. At the same time, however, the fleeting glimpses of Robert stalking the couple before they actually meet him suggest that the camera that we have relied upon so heavily in the opening scenes does not reveal everything, and we may be tempted to dismiss Robert in these scenes as merely an "extra." Later, of course, it becomes clear that he is stalking the couple, as his second appearance on camera should have alerted us.

When Robert does finally introduce himself to the couple, he lures them into his bar with the promise of the food and drink for which Colin and Mary are desperate. Clearly a master of the city, Robert fails to provide the couple with the nourishment that they crave, but, much like a cult leader, he offers sustenance of a different sort—his story and his propaganda. The means by which Pinter depicts this situation is nothing short of miraculous. Robert's voice literally leaves his body to hover over the bar while he tells his story. Unlike the traditional "reaction shots" of many films, during which a character's voice may continue while we witness the reaction of his or her listeners, Robert's voice remains disembodied for some time. What Pinter shows us is not the reaction of the listeners but the activities of the entire crowded bar. And, while other dramatists, notably Samuel Beckett, have used sound and silence for dramatic purposes, here and elsewhere (notably in *Mountain Language* [1989] and *Ashes to Ashes* [1996]), Pinter links this technique to situations that represent abuses of power.

The voice-over is particularly effective in this instance. Robert's voice and narrative permeates the bar, thereby implying his omniscient presence, as well as the catholicity of his narrative, a patriarchal story that transcends individuals but pervades culture like air. To highlight Robert's power, his voice reenters his body before our very eyes. At the same time, though, Pinter's technique illustrates the fact that what we are seeing in the bar, as well as what we are hearing from Robert, is, actually, a construct, subject to biases, interpretation, and manipulation. What we see in the bar is framed by Robert's narrative. It is here that the camera's power is presented at its most ambiguous; it has the power to move omnipresently, but because it is associated with Robert and his story, the screenplay makes it clear that it can also distort and oppress.

What we witness as Robert tells his tale is men—men talking, men drinking, men playing games together, images that prompt Ronald Knowles to conclude that we are in a homosexual bar (176). While the saloon is clearly a male domain, male relationships may not necessarily be homosexual in the physical sense. Instead, we may be witnessing a continental version of male bonding or, to use Irigaray's term, homosocial behavior. As is indicated in the McEwan novel, public displays of masculine affection are not uncommon in this locale (102). Interestingly, the bar that could be misread as a gay bar is Robert's ideal image of masculinity, a place where men are free to be men, a place free from the control of women.

Though Pinter indicates that several women appear in the bar, they are not a threat to the machismo culture. Using the sketchy descriptions from Pinter, Schrader creates two extreme and stereotypical representations of femininity—the virgin and the whore. Noticeably, the young woman listens adoringly while a man talks. Similar to the dissipated woman in Edgar Degas's *Absinthe* (1876), the other, older, woman sits alone watching the activities of the bar, perhaps the doyenne, perhaps lamenting the fact that she is no longer desirable on the sexual market. In both cases, the women appear to be placed in the position of spectators, generally a placement indicating power, but the camera's perspective on them, the camera that also carries Robert's voice, implies that they, too, are objectified. For example, the man whom the young woman listens to is shrouded in darkness; his identity and individuality are protected from the camera's gaze while hers is not. The camera diffuses any power that these women may have, and they are left silent. At the same time, however, Pinter's use of the camera and the voice-over reveals this female objectification underscoring the manner in which Robert and his narrative construct femininity. That is, while the camera objectifies women and prioritizes male perspectives, the screenplay makes this process and its inherent oppression apparent.

If there were any doubt about the patriarchal culture and Robert's intense participation in it, during the couple's stay at the apartment, Robert makes his views about gender explicit in words which Pinter takes almost verbatim from the McEwan novel:

> My father and his father understood themselves clearly. They were men and they were proud of their sex. Women clearly understood them too. Now women treat men like children because they can't take them seriously. But men like my father and my grandfather women took very seriously. There was no uncertainty, no confusion. (29)

Robert subsequently punches Colin in the stomach when the younger man characterizes his host's home and his masculine paraphernalia as "a museum dedicated to the good old days" (30).

Given these cultural markers, the novel and the screenplay may lead us to believe that the potential victim in the narrative will be Mary. In typical patriarchal narratives a man attempts to win, save, seduce, and overcome a woman in order to demonstrate his prowess. He is the actor; she is merely the means by which he demonstrates his ability to act. Initially, the film hints at such a conclusion. Robert seems interested in Mary in the bar, but, as is clear from the later scenes in which Caroline shows Mary the numerous pictures that they have surreptitiously taken of Colin, he is the object of their desire, the spectacle to be viewed to facilitate their voyeurism and ultimately their sadomasochism.

Colin, however, is not only objectified by Caroline and Robert. After the two tourists have spent several days engaged in intense sexual activity, which Pinter's script suggests is inspired by their contact with Caroline and Robert, they venture out into the mysterious streets of

Venice. They easily navigate their way to a restaurant where Mary comically asks Colin about people's preferences for breasts "thighs and bottoms." She questions Colin about the sensations of the objectified party, the inspiration for the comments: "When people look at you and . . . you know . . . talk about your thighs or your bottom or both, etc. . . . well, are you sensing them in the same way that they're sensing them. . . . To put it in a nutshell—when people talk about your thighs and bottom— what sense of your thighs and bottom do you, at such a time, have?" (34). Befuddled and bemused, Colin has no answer, but Mary implies that he should because "the whole damn restaurant is talking about your thighs and bottom" (35).

Of course, the scene demonstrates the couple's rediscovered interest in the erotic in a playful way, but it is significant that Mary questions Colin about the feelings of someone cast in the role of sexual object, again a violation of the stereotypical male role in speculation and narrative. Men are generally the voyeurs; women are at the mercy of their glances. Later, Mary's participation in this scene will also have great significance, but at this point, the screenplay underscores Colin's objectification by Mary, Robert, and the film. This violation of narrative and filmic tradition may be what makes *The Comfort of Strangers* so arresting; we are unaccustomed to viewing men as victims and objects of speculation.

In addition to its ramifications in regards to patriarchal narratives, Colin's objectification also provides for insights into the nature of Robert's interests in Colin. When he and Colin walk to the bar while Caroline drugs Mary at the apartment, Colin's role as object is highlighted again. In both the novel and the screenplay, a man pinches Colin while he is with Robert. And, when Robert and Colin enter the bar, Robert tells his other male friends that he and Colin are homosexual lovers.[2] Earlier in a scene that Pinter added, Robert declares that "society has to be protected from perverts. . . . [P]ut them all up against the wall and shoot them" (30). He implies that Colin is a "pouf" for disagreeing with him (31). Clearly, Robert uses homosexuality as a means of impugning Colin's masculinity, thereby underscoring Colin's status as an object, not a subject. Colin is just a plaything, like a woman, material for yet another narrative that Robert tells. And as the photos that Caroline and Mary have taken of Colin make clear, he has been figuratively captured on film prior to his literal victimization. Colin is at the mercy of Robert, his look, and even his language, for the men speak to Robert about Colin in their native tongue. Robert literally reconstructs Colin, making others see him differently.

In a later scene during which Robert murders Colin, this interplay among speculation, sexuality, and power is also illustrated. Robert may be attracted to Colin's beauty, inflamed by the opportunity to experience death through a sexual experience, or impassioned to kill with his wife Caroline watching. But, Robert's previous comments about Colin and men like him, the "poufs" that threaten male power, also suggest that Robert may believe that while he fulfills his sadistic sexual pleasures through the murder, he is also ridding the world of one weak man who symbolizes the larger threat to patriarchy. The fact that he is so confidently cool in the police station also suggests that he believes that no authority, no patriarch would blame him for the murder; he has merely exterminated a social problem. Again, Robert's sexual interest in Colin may have something to do with his ambivalent relationship to his own domineering father, it may represent his horror over his own homosexual tendencies (Hudgins, 56–57), or it may show that "patriarchal masculinity conceals a sexual ambiguity—which its owner then guiltily seeks to punish in others" (Billington, 318). Ultimately, though, his sexuality is about power, not men loving men. He wants to terrify and destroy whatever he sees. Through the murder, he gains complete control over another human being, literally objectifying Colin, making him a corpse. In this way, Pinter illustrates that the process of objectification is clearly a violent one. In the midst of beauty is blood.

Given this conclusion, it would seem that the relationship between spectator and spectacle is gruesomely oppressive. McEwan and Pinter, however, complicate such conclusions by having Mary watch the entire scene, a spectator watching participants creating a spectacle. Still, she is not just any spectator; she is a feminist viewer. In both novel and screenplay, clearly she struggles to define herself in terms of feminism and heterosexuality. She admires the radical feminists of the holiday city who rally to have rapists castrated. Her daughter has just made the all-male football team, and in the Pinter version she introduces herself to Caroline by her own name, while Caroline defines herself as "Robert's wife" (25).

More importantly, her representation as the object of speculation is more complex than the other female characters. She is not stereotyped, as the women in the bar are, and she seems to be curious about the entire process of objectification, as evidenced in her discussion of thighs and bottoms with Colin. Further, as an actress, a typically objectified position, she avoids traditional female representation by participating in an all-female theatre troupe. Tellingly, she admits that she has played in an all-women version of *Hamlet*. The reference, which appears in both the novel and the screenplay, cannot help but remind us of the opening sequence in the film, but it is also an important work to have mentioned specifically. It is, after all, a drama that has defined male careers for centuries. Further, it is about a person who chooses to act rather than be acted upon. Finally, in this vein, Mary admits that the theatre group has disbanded over arguments about the inclusion of male performers, so Mary now does voice-overs, a Pinter addition to the novel (27). The reference appears soon after Robert's own voice-over, so it is difficult to ignore the implications. Mary's unconventional participation in speculation, her role as an actress, her explicit sympathy with feminist issues, and finally her career as a voice-over artist usurps the patriarchal position of spectator.

The novelist and the screenplay writer both take pains to show that these challenges do not come easily for Mary. She clearly wants a relationship with Colin, but judging from her feminist comments, she is unwilling to settle for one that requires stereotypical gender roles. In both the novel and the screenplay, the source of her difficulties revolves around sexual intimacy. In the McEwan novel, the couple stops arguing about intellectual topics during the passionate phase of their holiday. Sexual fantasies replace discussions regarding the effects of gender and class on society. As Christopher C. Hudgins points out, however, McEwan's narrative comments make it clear that such complacency is disdainful and immature (61).

The Pinter screenplay includes no such comments, but, perhaps in a subtler way, Mary's children are used to illustrate the tensions between feminine independence and heterosexual intimacy. Although we literally never see the children, Mary's many references to them indicate that they are very important to her, while Colin's responses indicate that they are as incidental to him as they are to the McEwan novel (Tucker, 50). In a very startling way, Pinter uses motherhood, a culturally sanctioned role for women, as a means of violating patriarchal stereotypes. Rather than fulfilling male desires in some way, Mary's maternity complicates her relationship to Colin. In the screenplay, Colin, whom the novel tells us nurses at Mary's breast (90), frequently behaves like a spoiled child who is asked to share his mother's affections. And, when Caroline refers to him as a baby, Colin seems to protest too much that he is not (27). Tellingly, Colin's infantilism mirrors Robert's depiction of motherhood in his narrative. In that narrative, his mother reigns supreme, the only one in the family who does not abandon him, the only one who comes to him whenever he calls her to do so. For Robert, and perhaps for Colin, maternity is characterized by servitude. Any maternal power divorced from masculinity is threatening. As Robert tells Colin, "Now women treat men like children, because they can't take them seriously" (29).

For Mary, her maternity is her source of power, her anchor. Initially, Mary's motherhood and her confusion over its place in her relationship to Colin propel her into Robert and Caroline's world. After establishing Colin's indifferent and sometimes hostile attitude toward her children, Robert's interest in them seems refreshing. When she meets Caroline later, she struggles to define her relationship with Colin, while Caroline make it clear that loves means "that you'd do absolutely anything for the other person . . . and you'd let them do absolutely anything to you" (26). And though the perspective that Robert offers repulses the couple, they appear to be seduced by his certitude. It is after their first visit to the Venetian couple's home that they isolate themselves from the world and immerse themselves in narcissistic and erotic activities.

At this point, Mary's references to her children disappear in the screenplay, perhaps reflecting the disappearance of her own individuality. Significantly, McEwan has Mary exclaim after Robert has nursed her, "Why is it so frightening to love someone this hard? Why is it so scary?" (90). Mary responds to this intimacy by seeking solitude, the threat that they think will "destroy what they shared" (McEwan, 82). In both novel and screenplay, she swims into the ocean alone, an image that anyone who has read Kate Chopin's *Awakening* or Woolf's *To The Lighthouse* cannot but help as define as a feminist act. In any case, she is literally out of Colin's sight for a few moments, and when she returns in Pinter's version, she is clearly more independent. Colin proposes living with her and the children, but given his previous indifference to the children, as well as the nursing sequence in the novel, it is difficult to trust his motives here. He may, for example, be under the impression that erotic activities have displaced Mary's concern for her children. In the Pinter screenplay, it is clear that this is not the case, for Mary responds to his question as indifferently as he responded to her comments about her children earlier. Ultimately, she renounces the traditional patriarchal representation of heterosexual relations. Simply put, she seems to have reconciled her conflicts over her relationship with Colin and decides to live independently.

Soon after this decisive moment, she is drugged by Caroline, a completely male-identified woman, a woman who cannot believe that any action, in life or on stage, could occur without men (McEwan, 66–67;

Pinter, 27–28). Moments before the murder, in another self-conscious reference to speculation, Pinter has Caroline tell Mary, "We're on the other side of the mirror" (46). This allusion to the visual and Mary's clear violation of traditional female representation suggest that her position as a witness to the murder is a punishment for her challenges to the status quo. Under the influence of the drug, Mary wants to act but cannot, and what she sees as a narcotized spectator is the dark side of the erotic world that both she and Colin have misinterpreted as a solution to their own relationship problems. Robert and Caroline may have come to understand their relationship, seen their roles clearly defined, but the cost is high.

Mary survives the ordeal, but how and in what capacity varies between the novel and the screenplay. In the McEwan novel, for example, when the police question Mary, she does not say that she and Colin were going to be married (124), but in the Pinter screenplay she does (50). It would appear that in the novel Mary resists stereotypical characterization by the patriarchy while in the Pinter screenplay she accepts it. To complicate matters further, Pinter wrote an additional original scene to add to the film but due to time and talent constraints, the scene was never added. In it, Mary is happily reunited with her children (quoted in Hudgins, 68–69). Ironically, through the children, Mary can live independently.

As they stand, neither the novel nor the screenplay offers conclusive answers to questions regarding the characters' motives. Both manuscripts encourage audiences to continue speculating about the events. In the screenplay, however, one character appears to have an explanation. As Mary leaves the police station, she sees Robert behind a glass door telling the story of his life. She appears to escape, but Robert's narrative, his "museum piece," continues. On the one hand, this scene implies that escape from such patriarchal narratives is possible, but on the other, the screenplay ends, as it began, with an oppressive patriarchal narrative, one that continues despite challenges, one that appears to offer the security of an answer. As illustrated in the Pinter screenplay, however, such certitude is not only illusory but also violent and oppressive.

Such a conclusion illuminates many of the issues regarding speculation raised throughout the screenplay. Pinter presents the camera as both oppressive and liberating. As spectators, we cannot help but be disturbed by both Robert's sadistic use of speculation and Mary's narcotized participation in it. In a general way, Pinter may be cautioning his spectators about the seductive and potent power of the visual and moving image. His own experiences with the film industry, after all, have been mixed. As the Hudgins interview illustrates, there was literally more to *The Comfort of Strangers* screenplay than met our eye. The mechanism and the practical requirements of a film dictate its content. In a more diabolical way, the film moguls dropped Pinter as a screenwriter for a film version of Vladimir Nabakov's *Lolita*. He dryly responded by saying, "It's Hollywood" (Billington, 361). The industry, like Robert, controls narratives, their production, and the entire spectacle before us; despite their apparent veracity and seamless quality, they are, in fact, constructs, a difficult realization to keep in mind in a culture that prides itself on its verisimilitude so completely. The representation of the camera in this screenplay is not entirely Machiavellian, however, since Pinter has been able to challenge its supremacy while simultaneously using it to illustrate its very own intricacies.

NOTES

1. As Pinter scholar Martin Esslin made clear in his first full-length reading of Pinter, dramatists such as August Strindberg, Frank Wedekind, and Anton Chekhov create characters "who talk past each other rather than to each other" (209), but Pinter perfects the process not to "say that language is incapable of establishing true communication" but instead to draw "our attention to the fact that in life human beings rarely make use of language for that purpose, at least as far as spoken language is concerned." Martin Esslin, *The Peopled Wound: The Work of Harold Pinter* (New York: Doubleday, 1970), p. 212.

2. There is a slight variation between the novel and the screenplay during this scene. In Ian McEwan's work, Robert tells Colin, "Everyone we met, I told them that you are my lover, that Caroline is very jealous, and that we are coming here to drink and forget about her." Ian McEwan, *The Comfort of Strangers* (New York: Penguin, 1994), p. 104. In Pinter's, Robert tells Colin, "I was telling them [the men in the bar] you are my lover. And that Caroline is jealous because she likes you too." Harold Pinter, *The Comfort of Strangers* (London: Faber and Faber, 1990), p. 44.

CHAPTER SEVEN

⊞

On The Remains of the Day:
Harold Pinter Remaindered

EDWARD T. JONES

While Harold Pinter was offered co-credit for the screenplay of James Ivory's film version of *The Remains of the Day* (1993), the Columbia Picture's release of the Booker Prize–winning novel by Kazuo Ishiguro, he declined the offer. Therefore, Merchant-Ivory's usual collaborator, Ruth Prawer Jhabvala, alone, is credited with the successful film that enjoyed wide popularity and critical acclaim. To be sure, many of the best features of Pinter's unpublished screenplay seem to have been retained in the film,[1] but the essential integrity of the playwright's fidelity to Ishiguro, once more showing Pinter's penchant for time and memory, has been somewhat compromised by foregrounding the oblique love story that originally existed more as subtext of Stevens's missed moral and emotional opportunities both in Ishiguro's novel and in Pinter's screenplay. Pinter placed the latter-day action—putatively the present of the film—in 1954; Ishiguro's originally was set in 1956; Merchant-Ivory-Jhabvala chose 1958. This discrepancy causes no particular displacement in the narrative, yet the two-year variation among the several versions is curious.

Ishiguro uses first-person narration; however, the film and Pinter's screenplay open with voice-over from Miss Kenton, the former housekeeper, writing to her old coworker, Stevens, from Cornwall, where she has recently separated from her husband. Stanley Kauffmann faults the Merchant-Ivory-Jhabvala film for thus rupturing the first-person perspective of Stevens that he views as fundamental to the work itself:

> That perspective is not merely a literary device that could be discarded in the film. Ishiguro's aim was to show a man so encapsulated in protocols that all the major events of his life, political and emotional, happen on the periphery of that life. We see through his eyes, more clearly than he does what is happening around him. Ishiguro means this, I believe, as a comment on England. The film fractures his intent. (33)

In fairness, Merchant-Ivory-Jhabvala capture some of this effect with a subjective camera, although even then much of the emphasis is upon the male gaze directed at Miss Kenton from upper windows, porthole windows in the servant quarters, and, indeed, at one point, through a keyhole. The exchange of looks, stares, and glances provides the underpinning of the frustrated-love story of the film version at the expense of the political content that Ishiguro and Pinter underscore, most notably in the social criticism found in the novel.

The plot, such as there is, in Ishiguro's interior study and bittersweet comedy of manners (one might almost say "manors" as well) is familiar. Stevens, the chief butler, manifests inordinate pride and professionalism, duty and decorum, in serving Lord Darlington, who seeks to bring about respect and rapport among the European nations following the Great War. Jhabvala interpolates a scene not present either in Ishiguro's novel or Pinter's screenplay wherein Lord Darlington recounts the suicide of his German antagonist/friend after the war in which they both fought, a suicide committed because of the ruinous economic conditions imposed on Germany as a consequence of the Versailles Treaty. Darlington, on his way to becoming a person trapped in his own strategy, is determined to improve relationships before things further deteriorate. To this end the well-meaning, but diplomatically inexperienced, lord invites important figures from a number of governments to his manor to discuss the terms of a continued peace, a conference which inexorably leads to the duped lord subsequently being charged with appeasement and Nazi-sympathy. Stevens, out of loyalty and blindness, never seriously challenges his master's assumed rightness on these matters: "To listen to the gentlemen's conversation would distract me from my work," Stevens says late in the film by way of explanation for this complicity. Manners, like language, often because of seeming clarity, may actually hide relations that they support and on which they depend.

Not withstanding Stevens's moral ignorance, Ishiguro does permit him at least a moment or so of intellectual discovery in the novel, which Pinter echoes, although in a more reduced way, and Jhabvala omits altogether. In Ishiguro's novel, Stevens explains to a stranger whom he meets on the beach in Weymouth, a man who, as it happens, has also been in domestic service:

> Lord Darlington wasn't a bad man. He wasn't a bad man at all. And at least he had the privilege of being able to say at the end of his life that he had made his own mistakes. He chose a certain path in life, it proved to be a misguided one, but there, he chose it, he can say that at least. As for myself, I cannot even claim that. You see, I *trusted*. I trusted in his lordship's wisdom. All those years I served him, I trusted I was doing something worthwhile. I can't even say I made my own mistakes. Really—one has to ask oneself—what dignity is there in that? (Ishiguro, 243)

Pinter has Stevens say and poignantly repeat during this sequence on the beach, "I think I've given all I have to give. I gave it all to him, you see" (164). Early in his screenplay Pinter includes the discussion in the servants' hall about what constitutes a great butler to which Stevens contributes the one word *dignity*. Merchant-Ivory-Jhabvala eschew this exchange which prefigures much in Ishiguro's novel, including finally what measure of "discovery" Stevens can lay claim to. In the film the comment about his lordship's mistakes being his own which Stevens cannot acknowledge about his borrowed ones is spoken rather presumptuously and inexplicably by the man who gives the butler a lift to his stalled car in the West Country, considerably before the end of the film where it could serve as climax. Thematically this change appears the most damaging in capturing the letter and spirit of Ishiguro's novel.

Merchant-Ivory films are famous, or perhaps notorious, for their appreciation of texture and layers of caste as well as conventions. Yet somehow, contrary to what many believe, this aesthetic may get in the way occasionally of the content in their adaptations. Manchester-born author, John Ash, who celebrates Mike Leigh's *Naked* over the "tasteful" films of Merchant-Ivory-Jhabvala, writes apropos of their oeuvre but with special application to *The Remains of the Day*:

We know we should be attending to stilted pronouncements about democratic values and the fate of the Jews, but when the camera is falling in love with the drapes, it's kind of hard. (43)

This aspect receives particular attention in the montage sequence detailing the preparations for distinguished guests to visit in one of England's stately homes. The recurrent grand staircase with its vivid, nearly celestial, blue walls is used to good effect, especially the hidden door that yields access to the working underside of the house. Servants literally disappear into the woodwork, as Stevens likewise does metaphorically. This architectural feature represents a way to make servants always accessible but not inopportunely present. Although Pinter does not have this splendid detail in his screenplay, experienced filmgoers may remember something similar in the Losey-Pinter *The Go-Between* and the role of the staircase in the same collaborators' *The Servant*, both good text analogues to *The Remains of the Day*. Ash wonders whether the exaggerated respect that Americans give this kind of grandiose ambience and the film's special production values "might really be a symptom of a lingering colonial mentality" (43).

One nice detail is the shot in which Stevens is seen measuring the table setting with a ruler to make certain that each piece is precisely spaced according to some platonic ideal of butlerhood. Again, however, such detail further demonstrates Stevens' inability to move beyond the minutiae of housekeeping to larger substantive matters. Another beautiful setup reveals Stevens and Miss Kenton in silhouette as she tells him of his father's death, the deep blue of the staircase offering the only color. While Pinter does not specify any such effect in his screenplay, it is reminiscent of the momentary yellow screen of the Vermeer in his still unfilmed, but published, *The Proust Screenplay*.

Jhabvala strategically places scenes of romance as counterpoint to the unacted-upon attraction of Miss Kenton and Stevens. There is no parallel to these sequences in Pinter's more politically aware script. For example, in the film we see two servants, Lizzie and Charlie, exchanging kisses and amorous play on the lawn of Darlington Hall. Miss Kenton and Mr. Benn whom she agrees to marry, kiss passionately outside a pub on the housekeeper's night off. However well these interpolations work cinematically, they offer an emphasis that Ishiguro avoids in his novel and Pinter emulates in his adaptation. Both Ishiguro and Pinter are strongly unsentimental writers. In contrast, what has been filmed seems curiously sentimental, as if the content from the romantic novels that Stevens surreptitiously reads somehow has gotten transferred to the filmed adaptation of *The Remains of the Day*.

The particular scene in which Miss Kenton pursues Stevens's taste in books amounts to an apotheosis, and, for the most part, it is handled in the film as Pinter wrote in his screenplay. One detail that seems especially affecting in the film is the parallel of Stevens' prying away his stricken father's hand, finger by finger, from the old man's cart of mops and brooms and Miss Kenton's using the same gesture. Pinter writes in his unpublished script:

> *She* [Miss Kenton] *begins to take the book from him, lifting his fingers one at a time from the book. This takes place in silence, their bodies very close. She opens the book and flicks through it.*
>
> MISS KENTON: Oh, dear, it's not scandalous at all. It's just a sentimental old love story.
>
> *They look at each other.*
>
> STEVENS: I read these books—any book—to develop my command and knowledge of the English language. I read to further my education.
>
> *Pause.*
>
> MISS KENTON: Ah. I see. (103)

In the Merchant-Ivory film, Anthony Hopkins and Emma Thompson as the characters exchange pregnant glances during this sequence. The Jhabvala addition at the end of having Stevens say, "I must thank you not to disturb the few moments I have to myself" appears unnecessary, even a trifle jarring, in light of the romantic manner in which the sequence has been filmed. What Pinter makes an epiphany, in the film is qualified, which undercuts the romantic motives it has almost excessively cultivated.

One of the strangest alterations in the film for which there is no precedent in either Ishiguro or Pinter arises from discarding the American industrialist, Mr. Farraday, from the Ishiguro novel as the new owner of Darlington Hall and substituting, rather perversely, former Congressman Lewis as lord of the manor. Unlike Pinter, Jhabvala eliminates Ishiguro's disclosure about Lewis that the French delegate, M. Dupont in the novel and in Pinter's script, makes at dinner before proposing a toast to Lord Darlington. Pinter's version reads as follows:

DUPONT: But before I go on to thank our host, the most honourable and kind Lord Darlington, there is a small thing I wish to remove from my chest. Some of you may say it is not good manners to do such things at the dinner table.

Laughter.

But I have no alternative. I believe it is imperative to openly condemn any who come here to abuse the hospitality of the host and attempt to sow discontent and suspicion. My only question concerning Mr. Lewis is this does his abominable behavior in any way express the attitude of the present American administration? (69)

Thereafter, the film seems to follow the script as Pinter wrote it with Lewis's remark about "amateurs" rather than "professionals" in diplomacy and Darlington's retort that "what Mr. Lewis describes as 'amateurism' I would describe as honour" (Pinter, 71).

Jhabvala reassigns the comment about the evening being the best part of the day for many people from the stranger on the Weymouth beach to Miss Kenton, who appears in a brief sequence on the pier with Stevens, as the lights go on. The pair then take their leave with long-shot glances as she rides away on a bus in the rain, ending this extremely subdued brief encounter between the butler and the former housekeeper.

The film's ending returns us to Darlington Hall with symbolic overtones neither in Ishiguro's novel nor in Pinter's screenplay. Former Pennsylvania Congressman Lewis reminds Stevens that they are in the room where he confronted Lord Darlington and his guests during the conference in 1935. Characteristically, Stevens seems otherwise engaged and displays no shock of recognition. His immediate task is to rid the room of a trapped bird which, with a little encouragement, obligingly flies out an open French window in contrast to the caged Stevens, comfortably back in his butler's role, calm of mind, even his repressed passions spent. An aerial shot of the Darlington Hall exterior receding into the distance ends the film, parallel perhaps to the withdrawal of Miss Kenton—really Mrs. Benn—back to her formerly estranged husband and now pregnant daughter. Once more she is drawn back to life in contrast to Stevens's passivity and stagnation.

Because so much of Ishiguro's novel is implicative, these bolder, symbolic strokes at the end of the film fail to satisfy, despite the good intention that this producer-director-screenwriter team always display, in a manner, alas, somewhat reminiscent of Stevens himself. Pinter does not strain for much of an effect (or for Stevens' *affect*) at the end of his screen-play, thus remaining faithful thereby to Ishiguro:

> MAN [on the Weymouth Pier]: Listen mate. Take my tip. Stop look-ing back. Looking back'll get you nowhere. Why don't you look for-ward? Look forward to the evening. Believe me, it's the best part of the day. Honest. Take my tip. I know what I'm saying. The evening's the best part of the day.
>
> *The man stands.*
>
> See you again, then.
>
> *The man walks away.*

> The lights suddenly go on the pier. Cheers from the onlookers. Music starts from the pier through the loudspeakers. The crowd moves up the pier. Groups of girls and groups of boys call to each other. Some of them, laughing, chase each other through the crowd. Stevens sits still. He suddenly stands and looks at the brilliantly lit pier, gives a coin to the attendant in his booth, goes through the turnstile and walks away from the camera along the pier until he is lost in the crowd (164–65).

Stevens's loneliness is not merely the feeling of being companionless but the deeper terror of self-estrangement, something that Pinter's ending captures but the filmed version does not.

Georgia Brown's rather cruel, but accurate, assessment of the Mer-chant-Ivory film in *The Village Voice* proves apt:

> Merchant-Ivory-Jhabvala adapt by simultaneously reducing and blowing-up: summarizing, dropping complexities, relying on large performances, and finally sealing all in a garish, calendar-perfect visual envelope. What they intend, clearly, is elegance and decorum; what they dish up is high Kitsch. (60)

Without a completed film based on Pinter's screenplay, we cannot know, of course, how well it might have worked to bring Ishiguro's novel to the screen out of whole cloth. It, therefore, joins Pinter's *The Proust Screenplay* and his fine unfilmed script derived from Joseph Conrad's *Victory* as "movies" of and for the mind, if not for the eye, ear, and film industry. It belongs admirably in that distinguished company.

To an extent, Merchant-Ivory-Jhabvala appear to patronize Stevens in their film adaptation and, by indirection, perhaps the audience as well. Pinter exhibits sterner stuff in his version. The film may at first appear less condescending to Stevens by omitting the sequence from the novel where Spencer taunts the butler by asking his opinion on world economic issues and currency problems, to which Stevens politely replies, in Pinter's screenplay, "I can't help you sir, I'm afraid" (89). The passage in Ishiguro is extremely patronizing, as it was meant to be. It leads, nevertheless, to a significant revelation of Lord Darlington's character as subsequently he apologizes to Stevens for his guest's bad behavior and hints at Stevens's hitherto neglected moral insight via the butler's scrupulous memory. In the process both Stevens and Darlington are somewhat clarified. Pinter reproduces this encounter especially well:

> DARLINGTON: . . . But you see, Stevens, the thing was, Mr. Spencer had a point to prove to Sir Leonard. Sir Leonard had been talking a lot of old fashioned nonsense, you see. About the will of the people being the wisest arbitrator and so on. But the fact is, Stevens, democracy is finished. It doesn't work. What was it Mr. Spencer said last night? He put it rather well.
>
> STEVENS: He compared the present parliamentary system to a committee of a mother's union organizing a war campaign.
>
> DARLINGTON: Exactly. Look at Germany and Italy. They've set their houses in order. How? Through strong leadership. If you look at Italy and Germany you see something that *works*. None of this democracy rubbish there. (90–91)

The foregoing words from Pinter's screenplay are true to Ishiguro. We miss them in the film. Moreover, they attain a special resonance from Pinter because of his well-known and public espousal of fledgling democratic movements throughout the world and his indefatigable protests against political torture, oppression, and hypocrisy. Such issues as they appear in Ishiguro's novel are flattened in Jhabvala's screenplay, making the film seem more effete than its source material. In a cinema of the mind it is provocative to speculate on what Pinter's late collaborator, Joseph Losey, might have done with his friend's tougher, more direct, and less ornate screen treatment of *The Remains of the Day*.

"No man is a hero to his valet," say the French, and both Ishiguro and Pinter ultimately show that even someone like Stevens can discover why the more cynical French think as they do. Pinter cuts closer to the bone (and more deeply into Ishiguro's novel) in his adaptation than does Jhabvala. Pinter's usual intensity of purpose coupled with economy of means doubtless proved too antithetical to the method and aesthetic of Merchant-Ivory. Georgia Brown makes an astute point about Ishiguro's novel: "[It] may be overly schematic, but it is also strikingly ambitious in ways its detractors didn't pick up on" (60). Similarly, uncritical admirers of the Merchant-Ivory film may have missed the ambitiousness of Ishiguro's novel. Indeed, they have missed enough to suggest why Pinter dissociated himself from the project.

Not for the first time in his career has Pinter taken up the incomprehension between master and servant, the larger consideration of inter-class relationships, and the difficulty of meaningful action in the modern world. He, like Ishiguro, permits the English gentleman/butler to glimpse—out of the corner of the eye, as it were, occasionally with the shock of recognition—the evanescent and disturbing forms of twentieth-century politics and history, and then to go about his business, if he can. What is left over and left out from Pinter's screenplay in the Merchant-Ivory-Jhabvala production has been our subject here. The film is attractive and frequently persuasive, but it seems a diminished thing when compared to Ishiguro's novel and Pinter's adaptation. Maybe the last word should go to another Stevens, this time the American poet Wallace Stevens, who submitted that a "violent order is disorder," as well as the reverse; Harold Pinter understands that paradox in his unfilmed *The Remains of the Day*.

NOTE

1. Pinter gave me a copy of his typescript for his screenplay, which he revised January 24, 1991, during an interview that I conducted with him in London about his screenplays in May 1992, part of which appeared in "Harold Pinter: A Conversation" in *Literature/Film Quarterly*, XXI (1993): 2–9. In that interview, Pinter mentioned that Ishiguro liked the screenplay that he had scripted for a proposed film version of the novel. All references to Pinter's screenplay in the text are to this unpublished manuscript.

FIGURE 7. *The Trial.* Kyle MacLachlan as Josef K. addressing the court during the first hearing of his case before the Examining magistrate. The setting is the disused synagogue at Kolin, about 35 miles east of Prague. Europanda Entertainment and BBC Films. Courtesy of Louis Marks.

CHAPTER EIGHT

⊞

Producing The Trial: *A Personal Memoir*

LOUIS MARKS

The film does not go from dream to reality, as it were. It is *all*
reality or *all* dream. But one must remember that the knife
that is plunged into K's heart is real.

> —Harold Pinter, from a letter to the
> author accompanying the draft screenplay

I ended my talk on producing Harold Pinter's work to the Pinter Festival: An International Meeting at Ohio State University in 1991 with the words "Finally, having delivered the screenplay, Harold decided not to direct it himself." This had been his intention when he had first brought the project to me some years earlier and I had arranged for a script to be commissioned by BBC Films, but pressure from other commitments as well as a growing appreciation of the weight of the task involved brought a change of mind. It was a significant decision and much flowed from it.

In the months that followed, Harold and I considered other directors. It was not a long list. Some of those included were not available. Others passed—one gave as his reason that the script evoked no images in his mind. In late autumn 1989, we sent the script to the renowned Hungarian director and Academy Award winner Istvan Szabo *(Mephisto, Colonel Redl)*, whose stature as a European filmmaker with bitter personal experiences of living under both Nazi and Communist rule as well as having been nurtured by Franz Kafka (a writer banned by both regimes) seemed to make him an ideal choice. This time the response was immediate and enthusiastic.

Szabo, an *auteur* director, had always worked from his own material but was very positive about the screenplay and came to London to meet with my BBC colleagues and Harold. It was agreed that the production would start as soon as he had completed another film already scheduled for shooting the following spring.[1]

In the meantime, we would confirm the financing, start putting together a production team, and begin looking for locations in Budapest where Szabo had his own studio base and where we planed to do the shooting.

From our first meeting Szabo was definite about one thing: he wanted to cast Josef K as Jewish. He used to produce from his wallet a photograph of the young Kafka with his burning dark eyes and piercing intelligence and say "This is what I am looking for." In the months that followed, we looked at many actors. Eventually, as the date for production moved closer, Szabo broadened his search and, together with Harold and myself, finally agreed to offer the part to an interesting young American actor who was dark-eyed though not Jewish and seemed to have the right qualities, but by then other developments had occurred which bought our association to an abrupt end. This was in September 1991.

Our disagreements were essentially professional and not artistic, as has been inferred elsewhere.[2] Szabo's involvement with his other film extended well beyond the original deadline. Urgent decisions about our own production kept having to be put back, and the project was increasingly in danger of falling apart. The casting of other roles had to proceed if we were to meet our schedule, and still there was no certainty as to when the director would be available. Sadly, it proved impossible to agree on a realistic start date and, rather than drift on, we decided to look elsewhere.

With Szabo we had explored Budapest for locations but with limited results. On a flying visit to spokesman during this period, we became aware of far richer prospects. We had planned to film in both cities, but with Szabo no longer involved, it now seemed wholly logical and appropriate to film *The Trial* entirely in the city in which it had been conceived. With Czechoslovakia still tasting the fruits of its "velvet revolution" under Václav Havel, a new president who was a friend of Harold's as well as a fellow Kafka lover, the auguries looked encouraging. Havel took a great interest in our production, visited the filming and, in a discussion with Harold present, memorably exhorting us to "make it real."

Suddenly, the decision made two years earlier by Harold and me to set it realistically in its precise historic and geographic context of the pre-1914 Austro-Hungarian Empire in which the "worm" was already "eating away" took on an unexpected and exciting dimension. I remember vividly the thrill of discovery when we were taken to the vast main public transport depot on the outskirts of Prague to be shown a tramcar built around 1910. It still contained advertisements and theatre posters of the day and was in full working order and ready to roll out onto the streets of the old city. Kafka could well have ridden in it, and eventually in our film the two bank clerks Rabinsteiner and Kullich would peer disturbingly out of it at a tense Josef K making his way for the first time toward Juliusstrasse and the mysterious Court. By the time David Jones joined us as director in late 1991, we had fully committed ourselves to shooting in Prague. Jones had directed two of Harold's screenplays before (*Langrishe, Go Down* and *Betrayal*), and they enjoyed a close working relationship. The director's first step was to fly out with his production designer and begin looking for locations in this remarkable and remarkably preserved city.

Prague is a city of the unexpected, of deceptions. You turn a corner, go through a door, mount a stairway and reality seems to lurch alarmingly, defying "normality." Nothing is as you think it is. The doorway that we chose as the entrance to "48 Juliusstrasse," for instance, is of heavy oak set in a solid baroque stone building promising an entrance to an imposing residence. Not so. Disconcertingly, it opens directly onto a vertiginous run of stone steps leading down to an open courtyard surrounded on three sides by cheap working-class tenements shoddily thrown up in the late nineteenth century. There are cracked, plastered walls, outdoor toilets and rusty, iron-railed walkways. But, look up to the top floor and the last apartment to which K is directed in his hunt for the fictitious "plumber called Lanz," and we see that it is incongruously almost comically, dominated by an entirely inappropriate baroque stone façade suggesting the existence of a large and imposing interior, although its setting above such a humble dwelling seems almost capricious. Immediately, K's journey to the washerwoman's flat, from which an inner door opens joltingly into the vast courtroom, though bizarre, becomes wholly believable. In the same way Titorelli's studio, reached through another staircase in a different building, might just as credibly have a rear exit leading back into the court offices, which in turn, brings us back to the landing where the washerwoman lives. The "geography" of our film could be impeccable!

Thus, Prague, with its own Kafkaesque qualities displayed in solid brick and stone, made it possible in an uncanny way to follow Harold's injunction: "It is *all* reality or *all* dream." At the time, all of this seemed like extraordinary good luck. I say "seemed" because if the reality itself conveyed a sense of logic defied, then the boundaries between dream and reality become confused. Prague added an unexpected dimension, but I am not sure now if this is what Harold intended. His "or" might become "and," which could alter the perception. Of course, this is hindsight on my part.

I cannot recall now the discussions which led to our starting the film as we did. Harold's opening is of K asleep in bed. The murmur of men's voices from an adjoining room is heard. Then K's eyes open. We have no idea where we are. We only discover this slowly as the action develops. We discover it *with* K.

In the film we begin outside in a street in the city. We establish that it is early morning, a normal day: people going to work, café tables brought out and set up. Then the camera cranes up to show us a substantial apartment block of upper-middle-class turn-of-the-century stuccoed neobaroque grandeur moves to a window on the second floor and through it into a bedroom where we discover K in bed. Now the story begins. K wakes up and becomes aware of the old lady across the road peering at him with unusual curiosity. It gives him his first sense of unease. Somehow, though, since we have already established a normal workaday world outside, the impact is a bit defused. Unfortunately, something of the extraordinary power of the novel's opening lines has been lost.

Curiously, the process of achieving our opening threw up irritating minor problems, which should have alerted us to the main issue. It took many attempts, followed by another day's reshooting to get the shot to work. Very simply, if the street looked too busy it would indicate a later hour with the implication that K. was a late riser. Too quiet would say the opposite. It took time to get the balance exactly right. But, did it matter? Was the time not irrelevant? During the shooting, it seemed important to establish from the outset that the action was taking place in a real city, "in broad daylight."

Much later, in the final stages of postproduction, this opening proved problematic in another way. It began to concern me increasingly that neither script nor film referred in any way to the most famous sentence of Kafka's novel, the opening statement: "*Someone must have been telling lies about Josef K, for without having done anything wrong he was arrested one fine morning*" (7). Both the paranoia and the ambiguity of those words launch the book with exactly the right mix of unease and menace. Did the film need the text?

Harold, who has a deep-rooted antipathy to voice-overs, captions, or any similar superimposed devices, felt that the film stood up without it. It did not trouble him either way. David had shot the opening in a way that made it difficult to find a point where inserting the line would not be intrusive. For me, it was a matter of focus. After much discussion it was finally agreed to place the sentence over a blank screen immediately before the film began. Not the best solution to a problem, which worried me more than others.

In none of this do I mean to diminish the power of the opening sequence that we ended up with. For one thing, its "authenticity" is immaculate. And, as I watched it being filmed and got to know more about the building and the area, the building's appropriateness seemed remarkable. It stands in a district of Prague known as Josefov, the name given originally to the old Jewish quarter dating back hundreds of years, which had been largely leveled as part of a major slum clearance in the late nineteenth century. When Kafka was writing *The Trial*, the rebuilding was complete, but the district retained its Jewish character. All of Prague's historic synagogues remain as well as the ancient cemetery. For a time during this period Kafka lived in Pariski Street, one of the area's main thoroughfares. Even our café, I learned, was actually situated close to a real café of the period that Kafka had frequented. In a wholly unexpected way, we were filming in the reality that Kafka himself had inhabited.

Still, Prague did not yield all of the locations that we needed. The National Museum at the top of Wenceslas Square furnished the setting for a magnificent banking hall. The cathedral of Kutna Hora, forty kilometers east of Prague, became our cathedral, Prague's St. Vitus being in full-time service to foreign tourists who had suddenly discovered this intoxicating city and were pouring in by the tens of thousands.

The court offices proved harder, but we eventually gained access to a large, deserted building, cold and forbidding, which just happened to have housed the Gestapo headquarters during the Nazi occupation of

Prague. All of the crew found it an upsetting place to film in. Even without the Third Reich associations, it seemed to offer a depressing atmosphere of brutality and hopelessness. With this atmosphere there was an uncanny aptness in the selection of this building as the place where K first discovers that he is not alone in being accused and arrested for an unknown and unspecified crime. A "realistic" setting? The word continued to take on new layers of meaning for me.

The apartment of Frau Grubach, landlady to K, and Fraulein Burstner, among others, and lawyer Huld's house both required a specific relationship of rooms and passages which we were unlikely to find in the city, so we decided early on that we would have to build them in the Barrandov Studios where our production was based and where in those preprivatization days there was on staff a team of astonishingly talented and dedicated Czech craftsmen. The painter Titorelli's "wretched little hole of a studio" also had to be purpose-built. In the studio our designer, Don Taylor, added imagination and flair to embody the full flavour of the highly distinctive turn-of-the-century Prague style with its singularly rich embracing of art nouveau motifs. In particular, the use of quite brilliant *trompe l'oeil* effects to add to the heavy mystery and oppressive wealth of the lawyer Huld's apartment with its secret doors and dark, interconnecting passages served the film and the characters triumphantly. The evocation of the terror of the court offices in Bloch's recollections of his first sight of K when he encounters him again in Leni's kitchen provided just one instance of the seamlessness of the juncture between location and studio, which was one of the production's many achievements.

The location that proved most elusive and was far beyond our resources to build was also the most crucial, the courtroom where the accused K has his first—and only—hearing of his case before the Examining Magistrate. It had to be large and in unnerving contrast (for K) to its anteroom, but not so large as to strain belief. Again the solution came with its unexpected associations. Harold had been specific in our earliest discussions in insisting that, while overpowering and oppressive, the courtroom should be no more or less dream-like than the washerwoman's room, which serves as its anteroom. The reality/dream ambiguity should be a continuum. In practical terms, the courtroom also had to have a gallery and to be of a manageable size to fill to capacity. Kafka called it a "meeting, hall . . . quite packed with "a crowd of the most variegated people." The screenplay gives no description. The novel describes a gallery, also crowded.

In a sense, the first scene is more about the crowd and the hearing and less about the physical building. But, when K returns a week later, he finds the room deserted. This is when the washerwoman tells him of her intimate relationship with the Magistrate, and K's growing erotic interest in her is interrupted by the rapacious law student Berthold. Now the room takes on a character of its own. Kafka writes that it looked "even more sordid than on the previous Sunday," and there is an implication of decay and corruption.

After fruitless hunting in Prague with time almost running out, our Czech colleagues finally came up with a remarkable and somewhat disturbing find. They had located an abandoned synagogue in the old Jewish quarter of Kolin, a small Bohemian town about an hour's drive from the city. Earlier in the century, we were told, cousins of Kafka lived in an adjacent street in the ghetto, and he visited them on several occasions. Whether he ever visited the synagogue, this setting for our enactment of one of his most powerful scenes, is a matter of speculation. It is not impossible. It was unused in 1991 because less than 2 percent of the prewar Jewish population of Kolin survived the Nazi deportations to Terezin and the death camps. A handful returned after the war, but by 1955 the congregation had ceased to exist.

There are now no Jews in Kolin, and the synagogue belongs to the municipality, which, when we arrived, was about to start restoring the building to be used as a concert hall. Outside, the scaffolding was already in place. The interior, seen in our film, is virtually as we found it. In order to disguise the remains of the wooden Ark of the Law on the eastern wall, we stretched a length of old Hessian cloth. The delightful, primitive religious paintings on the other walls based on the tribes of Israel remained, but we were able to shoot round them. The cracked and worn timbers supporting the gallery where the women would have prayed and the rusted iron railing around the *bima,* or dais, in front of the Ark where the Law would have been read twice a week to the now vanished congregation, also needed no embellishment. Dust from the aged and crumbling plaster was disturbed by every movement and hung in the air as a kind of miasma. It was a perfect and wholly convincing setting, and I doubt that anyone who saw the film guessed at its true identity.

I doubt that knowledge of the building's past influenced Jones in deciding to populate the crowd at K's hearing with a significant number of extras dressed as Jews in Hassidic garb with long beards. We never discussed this. I only became aware of it on the actual day of shooting and argued strongly against it. There was no time to consult Harold, but I knew that this had not been his intention. In early discussions he had said to me that the crowd should be normal. This, too, was how Kafka describes it. He only singles out those in the front row as distinctive: "They were without exception elderly men, some of them with white beards." Harold was even bolder on this. "No beards," he said to me, lest they would bring a flavour of the grotesque, which he specifically wanted to avoid. In the novel there is a sense of almost patriarchal figures, "influential men, the men who could carry the whole assembly with them," but to characterise them as Hassidic Jews was open to misinterpretation of Pinter's let alone Kafka's meaning. (It also rather distracted from the other detail on which Kafka—though not Pinter—was very clear. In the novel all of the crowd wear badges, suggesting that they are members of some secret society. Our costume designer was punctilious in providing the small black badges, but they didn't really register.) David agreed to shoot the scene in a way to lessen the emphasis on the "Jewish" faces, and in the later editing this aspect was somewhat more reduced, yet the strong effect of such clearly definable iconic figures was impossible to remove significantly, and it remains for me a blemish on the film.

If there are Jewish elements to be found in *The Trial,* they need to be very carefully considered. Simply to insert a Jewish presence into the courtroom crowd seemed to me to confuse a discussion that it would have been preferable to ignore rather than introduce in this way. Can it be ignored? Not, I think, if it relates to one of the most important questions we had to address: Who is Josef K? This is a question that Kafka left to the reader, to paint in whatever face he or she wants—or not. On the contrary, film has to define, to put something in the empty space. And willy-nilly, this becomes part of the "text." The audience "reads" a face and responds to it.

It is no secret that the casting of K proved the most difficult problem of the entire project. Although not a big-budget movie, *The Trial* was by no means cheap to film. An authentic period piece never is. Its cost was unlikely to be recouped by a purely art house release. However, to break into the mainstream, we would need a star actor. Our backers, who were men of total integrity and had responded to Harold's screenplay with unquestioned enthusiasm, believed that it was possible to make a film of integrity which could also work at the box office. What kind of film would this be? And, what kind of man was its hero?

All kinds of different and complex factors were at work here, starting with the screenplay. Harold maintained the ambiguity of the novel. K was simply K. He has no background, no pedigree, no religion (he crosses himself on seeing the Priest in the cathedral, but that could just be out of politeness or embarrassment), no political views, no defined social circle. He is undefined by any friendships. All we know for certain about him is that he is thirty years old, a bank clerk, living alone, and unmarried.

Our backers had no problem with this. Indeed, they saw it as a positive advantage to the film's commercial potential. If K were simply any up-and-coming young man who works in a bank and one day wakes up to find that his world is suddenly falling apart with everyone around him seemingly conspiring to destroy him, our film could surely have immediate meaning for his equivalent in today's high-pressured, get-rich-quick-world of yuppiedom and endemic insecurity with power wielded by vast, unidentifiable conglomerates whose orders are often unexplained, inexplicable, but absolute. A whole generation of men and women worldwide could identify with Josef K. To make him a true hero, he must not be simply a victim but has to be seen to fight back against his accusers rather than weakly submitting to his fate, even if in fighting back, he only manages to dig himself deeper into the pit. In an interview in Prague during the filming, Jones clearly emphasized the modern relevance of K's situation.[3]

Considerations of this kind eventually led us to the casting of Kyle MacLaughlin in the lead role. I think it was his positive, clean-cut, unsentimental quality that most influenced the choice. There would be no danger of self-pity, and he could personify a clear-eyed combative intelligence, combined with a star quality, which would make his growing awareness of the hopelessness of winning his case all the more shattering. MacLaughlin delivered everything that was asked of him. Especially in the later scenes, in his confrontations with Huld and the Priest, he gives powerful and anguished expression to K's determination to preserve his own integrity, even while all avenues of hope are closing against him, and the inevitable end looms.

Ultimately, though, he never quite managed to make the film *about* Josef K. In all of the confrontations that make up the film, the *other* person somehow manages to dominate. In her brief but perceptive article on the film, in *The Pinter Review: Annual Essays 1994*, Jeanne Connolly does not even mention him, although her comments on some of the other performances show a strong awareness of the key role of the "bravura performances" in contributing to the film's achievement. Connolly is right: we were wonderfully served by our actors. Michael Kitchen's Bloch,

Alfred Molina's Titorelli, Polly Walker's Leni, Anthony Hopkins's Priest and—among the lesser roles—Douglas Hodge's Inspector and Patrick Godfrey's Court Usher, all enlarged and enriched the text as wholly believable characters while staying within the powerful dynamic of the drama. They remain vividly in the mind. Despite this and the subtle tensions of the screenplay, Connolly concludes that the film "stops just short of being compelling."

I have pondered over this situation in the five years since the film was released to, one must admit, limited commercial and critical success. The power of the "nightmare" that enmeshes K at every point of his existence is, I have no doubt, excellently conveyed through the taught relentlessness of the Pinter screenplay and the crystal clarity, uncluttered by any indulgence of emotion or effects, of Jones's direction. It is also distinguished from any other attempt to film the work—and most of all from the Orson Welles version—by Pinter's fidelity to his source. I like to think that Kafka would have recognized his work here. Also, those who come fresh to Kafka will find much to deepen their understanding. In particular, the strong eroticism and considerable humor of the book, often sadly lost on readers who come to it with an over-reverential mind, found rich expression.

The film also closely reflected Harold's own intentions in the screenplay about which he had written:

> *What I found absolutely natural was to tell the story straight, as it were, as a hard, taught, objective series of events. The narrative is in itself remorseless and inevitable. It needs no embellishment or manipulation. I have a sense of a constant and implacable force behind it, a constant and implacable presence.*

This was achieved. The screenplay conveys the essence of the book brilliantly. The film set it in a real world, time, and place. But is this finally possible without some loss?

So much of Harold's work seems best realized when it is firmly rooted in recognizable reality. His own productions of his plays reveal a degree of truth and humanity and humor that distinguishes them strikingly from their sometimes more ponderous and "significant" effect in other hands. To set *The Trial* in a real, recognizable world, then, makes total sense. The flogging scene is not a flight of fevered imagination. There is no normal, reasonable world. Violent, unreasoning brutality (though it does, of course, come with its own perverse logic) is part of real experience.

But once one starts to recreate that "real" world, other questions crowd in. Reality has to be perceived. Is there not always the danger of selectiveness, of omission? We have a received image of pre-1914 Austro-Hungarian Empire that is, in Harold's words, "an apparently solid structure in every way—the buildings, the furniture, the money, the attitudes, and so on—within which there is a worm eating away." There were, naturally, of course many worms, the most voracious of which had a name—anti-Semitism—and was to end up disintegrating the very foundations of European civilization in ways that we are still trying to comprehend. Certainly it was already rampant at the very heart of the empire, Vienna, and Kafka wrote bitterly about its widespread presence in Germany in the 1920s. No one is more conscious of the role this was to play than Harold. "I was brought up in that territory," he said in an interview that he gave in Prague while visiting the filming. The territory that he shared with Kafka was an awareness of the victims of the new forces in Europe: "I was a child of the thirties . . . I was well aware the Gestapo. I'm also Jewish—so was he, by the way, so there's a link there too." Of course, many other worms are at work, eroding the structures and laying bare the darker and more atavistic sides of human nature. It would be grotesque to characterize *The Trial* as a work concerned only with specifically Jewish unease in this emerging world; it would also be a distortion to say that played no part.

In the same interview, Harold stated that he thinks that the novel:

> is actually about man's relation to God, and therefore if you follow the terrible tricks—the stumbles that happen in the whole work, then one has to ask what is God up to. Isn't that what the book is actually asking? What kind of game is he playing? I think that's what Kafka is asking and there is no answer. (Billington, 348)

This is a profoundly Old Testament view. The Israelites time and again bitterly asked God why he had dragged them out of Egypt to suffer hunger and death in the desert rather than leave them where they were safe and comfortable. In response, God becomes angry, and it takes all of Moses's powers of persuasion to get Him to relent. How would He look, Moses argues, if He broke his promises to the people whom He had chosen for his work? The Old Testament God is petulant, touchy, not altogether unlike the beings He has created. He is all-powerful, yet not above criticism. He even gets it wrong sometimes. Jewish railing against God's unfairness is part of folklore and is echoed in this century in the story of Auschwitz prisoners putting God on trial for allowing this suffering to continue and concluding after several days of hearing the evidence that He was guilty. This image of God playing dangerous games with humanity is profoundly Jewish, part of a culture that both Pinter and Kafka share.

But, to come back to the question of why our film, so excellently realized in most ways, failed to compel an audience. My hunch, and—as Harold admitted of his own theory about *The Trial*—it can never be proved either way, is that part of the problem was our failure to give K a truly recognizable identity. I think that K needed to be recognizable in himself so that an active chemistry could have been established with the audience, deepening their involvement. And if a specific identity, then why not Kafka's own? It might have introduced a subtext to which an audience could connect.

As excellent as MacLaughlin's performance was, he could not overcome the essential and literal anonymity of the character. Why does he not even have a name? It is difficult to care about the fate of a cypher, and this is what our film essentially was asking its audience to do. Perhaps something of the universality of the novel may have been lost, but not as much as one might think. Universality can often express itself as blandness, as generality, whereas identity can be sharp-edged, provocative, and exciting and not deny the wider universality of the experience. Harold does not see *The Trial* as a prophetic work. Yet, had Kafka not died in 1924 but lived on in Prague for another seventeen years, he would have suffered the same fate as virtually all of Prague Jewry—writers, artists, musicians, bank clerks as well as those members of his family who are commemorated on his own grave—who died "like dogs" for no other crime than having been born. Some of them in stone quarries.

These were my thoughts during those weeks in Prague as Kafka's nightmare world was brought to life. I don't think that anyone else on the production shared them, and I think that the film finally was faithful to Harold's intentions.

NOTES

1. *Meeting Venus*, a satire on international collaboration in the arts, built around a multinational opera production.

2. Michael Billington's account, *The Life and Work of Harold Pinter* (London: Faber and Faber, 1996, p. 348), is incorrect in many particulars. Pinter was not commissioned to write a screenplay for . . . Istvan Szabo." There was no director in mind at the time of commissioning other than the possibility of his directing it himself. Billington writes that their ideas about the film were "irreconcilably opposed." This grossly misrepresents the situation, as, indeed, does the statement that Szabo "wanted Josef K to be seen as the archetypal Jewish victim and wanted to outdo Orson Welles in cinematic Expressionism." As to the latter, Szabo accepted the screenplay and the historical "realistic" setting, and while some of his other work shows great interest in symbolism, he is not widely considered an Expressionist. On the question of the Jewish casting that Szabo wanted for Josef K, it is presumptuous to extrapolate the prejudicially loaded "Jewish victim" epithet. Szabo wanted to build on the image of Kafka himself, who was Jewish but could in no sense be called "archetypal." Billington's statement that "in 1992 the project passed into the hands of BBC Films with Louis Marks . . . as producer" is also misinformed. It had all begun eight years earlier when Harold brought the idea to me as a producer who had worked with him on other projects in the BBC Drama department, a part of which was later launched as BBC Films.

3. This interview, as well as untransmitted parts of the Pinter interview referred to below and interviews with other members of the production, is preserved in the Independent Television News tape archives in London, and I must express my gratitude for being granted access to these archives while preparing this article.

CHAPTER NINE

⊞

Harold Pinter's Lolita: *"My Sin, My Soul"*

CHRISTOPHER C. HUDGINS

In the fall of 1994, Steve Gale and I spent several weeks in London studying the sixty-four boxes of material in the new Harold Pinter Archive in
the British Library. We also passed a delightful two hours with Mr. Pinter in his study, where he told us how much he had enjoyed writing a
filmscript for Vladamir Nabokov's *Lolita.* Somewhat later, and to my surprise, I discovered that the project was brought to him by Adrian Lyne,
the director of *9½ Weeks, Fatal Attraction,* and *Indecent Proposal* (Letter,
March 13, 1995).[1]

During our conversation, Pinter commented that, on one level,
though the novel is about child abuse, in the 1962 Stanley Kubrick film,
"we barely see them touching." Any film true to the spirit of the novel, he
went on, must deal with that matter. He added that the novel has a "voice
the like of which has never been heard before," referring to the subtle,
complex first-person narrator which Nabokov brilliantly creates. Pinter
told us that the director had wanted him to use a good bit of narrative
voice-over to capture that complexity, but he emphasized that he chose to
use as little voice-over as possible. Seemingly very pleased with his script,
at this point he was concerned that it might not be produced, both
because of potential financing problems and because of what he called the

123

current atmosphere in Hollywood. He had spent six months on the script, Pinter said, adding that it includes a good deal of humor. He agreed with me that the Kubrick version had gone over the top in this regard, particularly in the Shelley Winters and Peter Sellers segments.

Soon after my return from London, Pinter sent a copy of his *Lolita* script along with a suggestion that I comment on it (Letter, November 11, 1994). In response to my lengthy reply, I was delighted to get back a gracious letter of thanks, which included this line: "I gather David Mamet has been brought in, whether this means he'll start afresh I have no idea" (Letter, January 23, 1995). Mamet also kindly sent me his version of *Lolita.* The Pinter script is dated September 26, 1994; Mamet's carries a March 10, 1995 date on the final page. Tracking an intriguing progression of scriptwriting, through circuitous trails I obtained two other scripts. The first, by James Dearden, who wrote *Fatal Attraction* for Lyne, is dated October 21, 1991. My copy of the script by Stephen Schiff, the one from which Lyne shot, is dated July 6, 1995. Schiff, a staff writer for *The New Yorker* and other magazines, has no previous scripts to his credit.

No doubt Lyne's reasons for rejecting the first three scripts that he contracted would be revelatory. Indeed, these four adaptations of a masterpiece are quite revealing on their own. My primary interest, here, though, is in the Pinter script, the best of the four, a masterpiece in itself as a model of subtle, aesthetically pleasing adaptation.

Such details as are available paint an interesting, if only partial, picture of Lyne's progression through those four scripts. The author of a wrongheaded and shallow article in the *Los Angeles Times* of June 10, 1990 comments on the Dearden script, noting that Carolco paid one million dollars to the Nabokov estate for the rights (Mitchell and Wilson). The authors maintain that the 1962 film's epilogue about Humbert dying of a heart attack is a sop "in observance of the prevailing Hollywood moral code." In a *New York Times* article from April 19, 1991, Dearden comments that Lyne had long wanted to direct his version of *Lolita* (Van Gelder). Dearden is still mentioned as the writer as late as April 26, 1993 in an article suggesting that *Lolita* may have a "pay for view" broadcast before theatrical release (Busch). In the June 20, 1994 *Hollywood Reporter* it is noted that "Harold Pinter is rewriting James Dearden's screenplay for Carolco's remake of *Lolita*" (Anonymous, "The E-Mail"). Pinter is again cited as the author in an October 27, 1994 article on Carolco's "firesale" due to its troubled finances (Fleming). In the December 5, 1994 *Hollywood Reporter* the news is broken that Chargeurs, a French textile and media conglomerate, bought the rights to both *Lolita* and *Showgirls* from Carolco in its attempt to make films that will reach a global audience (Farrell).

An article in the January 26, 1995, *L.A. Life* contains the information that "Producer Richard Zannuck reported that after drafts of the screenplay were written by James Dearden and Harold Pinter, David Mamet tackled the job and is wrapping up what Zannuck and director Adrian Lyne are confident will be the final script" (Anonymous). Finally, in a July 14, 1995 article in the *Los Angeles Times*, all four writers are listed, with the note that Schiff's is the shooting script, with filming to begin August 15 in Texas, Louisiana, and North Carolina and citing a projected completion date of November 1. Lyne comments in this article that the latest script "is punched up with more sex scenes and black humor" (Brennan, F14). Along the way, for the central role of Humbert Humbert, Dustin Hoffman, Hugh Grant, Kevin Kline and Daniel Day-Lewis were all mentioned as serious possibilities. Actually cast are Jeremy Irons as Humbert, Melanie Griffith as Charlotte Haze, and Dominique Swan, recently celebrating her fifteenth birthday, as Lolita; she has a body double for the sex scenes. Frank Langella plays Quilty.

In his letter to me dated March 13, 1995, Pinter writes, "My contract states that the film company can bring in another writer but that in such a case I can withdraw my name, which is exactly the case with 'The Remains of the Day.'" During our 1994 interview, Pinter told Gale and me that he had learned his lesson after the revisions imposed on his script for *The Handmaid's Tale*, which he has decided not to publish. When his script for *Remains of the Day* was radically revised by the James Ivory–Israel Merchant partnership, he refused to allow his name to be listed in the credits. We did not see Pinter's name up in lights when Lyne's *Lolita* finally made its appearance in 1998. Pinter goes on in the March 13 letter to state that "I have never been given any reason at all as to why the film company brought in another writer," again quite similar to the equally ungracious treatment that he received in the *Remains of the Day* situation. He concludes that though he never met Nabokov, "indeed I knew 'Lolita' very well and loved it."

Pinter has commented that in his adaptation of novels for films he attempts to remain faithful to the spirit of the novel while still retaining the freedom to seek out creative, aesthetically pleasing ways to transfer that spiritual core of the work from page to screen (1984 interview with the author). That process often necessitates some degree of artistic license.

Still, his *Lolita* script is the one of the four that is most faithful to the spirit of Nabokov's novel. Opinions about just what is central to that wonderful, complexly ambiguous work certainly vary. I would argue that Nabokov implies significant moral growth in both Humbert and in Lolita against a darkly humorous backdrop indicting our society, but it is the subtle depiction of that moral growth which makes the novel more than a titillating appeal to our prurient interests or to our "easy," socially critical liberal instincts. In addition, an aesthetically complex and evocative portrait of love and rapture and a subtle advocacy of a courageous exercise of free will in the face of mortality define what is best about this novel, arguably one of the major achievements of twentieth-century fiction.

In a famous essay, Lionel Trilling points us in this direction. He suggests that the novel is not about sex but about love, that is, the romantic, passionate love that cannot long exist in marriage. Commenting on Humbert's stated purpose, "to fix once for all the perilous magic of nymphets," Trilling goes on to note that "nymph" is Greek for "marriage," which passionate love aspires to but which destroys it. He puzzles over Humbert's declaring his love late in the novel for the older, very pregnant, domesticated Lolita and suggests that one of several viable readings is that Humbert has grown morally and repents his past vile sins (11).

In one of the best recent commentaries on *Lolita*, David Rampton argues that neither of the two prevalent critical responses to the novel is central. The first includes work that annotates and deciphers literary allusions, Nabokov's language puzzles, and so on, often pointing toward some vision of the aesthetic as central to the novel's themes. The second suggests that the "ostensible subject" of *Lolita* is not the real one, that the novel is really about American values, the immortality of art, and the aesthetic response to death. Arguing that actually the human drama of the story is central, Rampton maintains that the author calls on the reader both to condemn Humbert and to sympathize with him. He suggests that a viable response to such ambiguity depends on the dramatized scenes, those without narrative comment. Like Trilling, he emphasizes Humbert's last meeting with the pregnant Lolita, which points to both Humbert's growth and to Lolita's (110–11).

These dramatic scenes are precisely where the strength of Pinter's adaptation lies. In both novel and script, Humbert's essentially unmediated appeal that Lolita come and live with him as wife, not nymphet, his giving her inheritance with absolutely no sexual strings attached, as she thinks at first there will be, his directness of emotion for this much changed, domestic Lolita, all stand in contradiction to his previous behaviors (Nabokov, 252–54). Humbert has often recognized those previous behaviors as reprehensible, but he indulged his horrific proclivities anyway, implicitly blaming his pedophilia on his fixation on Annabel Leigh, volume of Edgar Allen Poe in hand, who died soon after their almost consummated adolescent tryst. As he says in the novel, he only manages "twenty-four years later to break her spell by incarnating her in another" (17). Complicating this psychological self-portrait further, Humbert also reports that his "very photogenic mother died in a freak accident (picnic, lightning) when I was three"(12). Pinter chooses to omit this element.

Rampton reads Humbert as understanding that Lolita has grown morally by making the decision to leave Quilty and work her way toward maturity through a series of menial jobs and a responsible, if unromantic, marriage with Dick Schiller (111–12). Humbert concludes that by rejecting him and settling for a potential life of drudgery with a husband and a baby, Lolita has made a choice which is good, even though it hurts him to the point of near hysteria (252–54). For Rampton, one of the book's finest moments is when Lolita refuses to recount the particulars of her debauchery with Quilty with that baby in her womb, which Humbert comments to himself "made sense" (112). Such a scene, Rampton observes, "doesn't 'solve' the problem of *Lolita*; the issues raised by the novel are not the kind that anyone ever resolves. But it does remind us why *Lolita* matters, and why we go on talking about it" (113).

Arguing against feminist reassessments, Zoran Kuzmanovich goes a step further, suggesting that at his core Humbert is obsessed with "the decay and death of the body, his body, Lolita's body, . . . all bodies" and that "in those fears, which we seldom express and always in moments of deepest polar privacy, we may very well identify with him." He concludes that "*Lolita* . . . at some deep level [is] an effort of generous and compassionate art to comfort us about our fears of death" (9, 10).

In his rich novel Nabokov recounts many recognitions on Humbert's part that suggest such moral growth through confrontation. As they leave the hotel where they have spent their first night together, after consummation, Humbert muses: "More and more uncomfortable did Humbert feel. It was something quite special, that feeling, an oppressive hideous constraint as if I were sitting with the small ghost of somebody I had just killed" (129). Gradually, Humbert ceases to see pedophilia as his inheritance from "the patrimonies of poets" (121) and begins to understand it as a "sterile and selfish vice" (253). He eventually regards his first masturbatory experience on the couch with Lolita as a horrific part of his life, "all that I now canceled and cursed" (253). He recognizes that he has robbed Lolita of her adolescent experiences with boys (170), and that she would have become a champion at tennis had he not broken something in her (212). In a central passage, as the older Humbert meditates with a priest about his experience, he comments:

> I had hoped to deduce from my sense of sin the existence of a Supreme Being. . . . Alas, I was unable to transcend the simple human fact that whatever spiritual solace I might find . . . nothing could make my Lolita forget the foul lust I had inflicted upon her. Unless it can be proven to me—to me as I am today with my [diseased] heart, and my beard, and my putrefaction—that in the infinite run it does not matter a jot that a North American girl child named Delores Haze had been deprived of her childhood by a maniac, unless this can be proven (and if it can, then life is a joke), I see nothing for the treatment of my misery but the melancholy and very local palliative of articulate art. To quote an old poet:
>
>> The moral sense in mortals is the duty
>> We have to pay on mortal sense of beauty. (258)

Finally, late in the novel two evocative scenes underline Humbert's recognition of what he has done to Lolita. Remembering one of Lolita's less attractive friend's innocent relationship with her father, he comments on Avis's comforting Lolita when she cuts herself with a fruit knife: "Avis who had such a wonderful fat pink dad and a small chubby brother, and a brand new baby sister, and a home, and two grinning dogs, and Lolita had nothing" (260). Humbert links this scene to his memory of Lolita's asking after her "murdered mummy," and his failure to comfort her while she reads a book about a child who has lost her mother: "Now, squirming and pleading with my own memory, I recall that on this and similar occasions, it was always my habit and method to ignore Lolita's states of mind while comforting my own base self" (261–62). And, as he reminisces about his own mother's accidental death by lightning, he concludes:

> But the awful point of the whole argument is this. It had become gradually clear to my conventional Lolita during our singular and

bestial cohabitation that even the most miserable of family lives was better than the parody of incest, which in the long run, was the best I could offer the waif. (262)

The second of these scenes follows Humbert's murder of Quilty as he awaits the police; he remembers a day soon after Lolita's leaving him when he has contemplated a valley from a similar hill where he "stood, wiping my foul mouth." Humbert recognizes that the sound that accompanies his contemplation of a glorious natural setting

> was but the melody of children at play, nothing but that, and so limpid was the air that within this vapor of blended voices, majestic and minute, remote and magically near, frank and divinely enigmatic—one could hear, now and then, as if released, an almost articulate spurt of vivid laughter, or the crack of a bat, or the clatter of a toy wagon. . . . I stood listening to that musical vibration from my lofty slope, . . . and then I knew that the hopelessly poignant thing was not Lolita's absence from my side, but the absence of her voice from that concord. (280)

Despite Lyne's decision not to use it, the Pinter script is the best of the four aesthetically. Lyne's choice of a script that "punches up" the comic and sexual elements of this masterpiece surely has more to do with his own sensibilities and with hoped for box office popularity than with good aesthetic judgment. In the first place, Pinter's ear for dialogue is a refreshing change from Dearden's ham-handedness and better than either Schiff's or Mamet's. Pinter's script also renders Humbert's reality complexly, in parallel with the fruitful ambiguity of Nabokov's original, and his structuring of the adaptation creates an effect similar to the suspense and complicated foreshadowing that Nabokov uses to amplify on Humbert's thematic musings about fate and free will.

For example, Pinter opens his script in the dank little town of Coalmont, Illinois, where Humbert has gone to find Lolita and her husband near the end of the novel. As we watch him ask directions of two women outside a grocery store, we hear in voice-over Humbert label himself a moral leper, not a nice man, abnormal. He adds: "Don't come any further with me if you believe in moral values. I am a criminal. I am diseased. I am a monster. I am beyond redemption" (1). He opens his car's glove box, puts the revolver he finds there in his jacket pocket, and then picks up a bobby pin, blows dust from it, and places it back in the glove box.

The effect of this structural decision on an audience is typically complex, almost as much as in *The Go-Between* or in *The French Lieutenant's Woman*. Largely drawn from "Dr. Ray's" fictional preface to the novel, that labeling voice-over both emphasizes Humbert's depravity and ironically implicates the audience in that depravity—unless it gets up and leaves, it follows Humbert along, an implicit questioning of its moral values given his advice not to come for this ride. Humbert's statement that he is beyond redemption both reflects his feeling at this moment and ironically foreshadows a recognition of his own moral growth at the end of the Pinter script, which still echoes the wonderful ambiguity of Nabokov's often unreliable narrator.

The Kubrick version begins with Humbert's driving through fog to Quilty's mansion; the Schiff version begins in Humbert's car after he has killed Quilty. Both Mamet and Dearden begin their scripts in mental institutions. Pinter's choice is better in that it immediately centers our interest on the crucial reunion scene and its implications of both Humbert's and Lolita's moral growth. Unlike the other scripts, it also maintains the novel's suspense about who it is that Humbert plans to kill. *And,* it avoids the caricature that flaws the tone of the Kubrick film from the start.[2]

As Humbert approaches Lolita's door, Pinter uses voice-over once more, the Lo in the morning lines from the novel, emphatically in the past tense: "Lo. Lee. Ta. . . . She was Lo, plain Lo, in the morning, standing four feet ten in one sock. She was Lola in slacks. She was Dolly at school. She was Dolores on the dotted line. But in my arms she was always Lolita" (2; 11 in novel). Pinter's placing these lines from the novel's opening at the beginning of Humbert's moral recognition scene with the dowdy, pregnant Lolita emphasizes, indirectly and subtly, the contrast between "early" and "late" Humbert, underlines that he has grown, that he is in love, now as never before, with a woman who has matured beyond nymphet status. Still, he goes on to show Humbert at the door, his hand in his pocket. But as our suspense mounts as to his likely target, Pinter cuts to a mimosa grove where the fourteen-year-old Humbert ardently searches beneath Annabel Leigh's dress while the grownups play their game of poker (3).

Their dalliance interrupted, Pinter cuts to a scene on the beach where Annabel's hand pursues Humbert's thigh in the sand. This visual paraphrase of the novel's description makes clear that Annabel, like Lolita, is sexually aggressive at a tender age. Pinter then cuts to the cave and a shot of a pair of sunglasses perched on a rock. The youngsters have managed to get out of their clothes, but they're interrupted by two bearded bathers who stumble upon them (5). As in the novel, the script includes echoes from this scene that comment on Humbert's and Lolita's later being discovered making love in another natural setting, much to their embarrassment.

When the young Humbert gets the news of Anna's death by typhus from his father, he gets no answer to his real question, "Why did she die" (6), but only the facts of the disease and the place of her death, in Corfu. Pinter's succinct description of Humbert's reaction to a death that he does not understand works well, especially with the cut to the Ramsdale Rail Station that immediately follows. When we cut to Charlotte Haze's home, Pinter's version implies a connection between the Annabel Leigh cave sequence and the "modern" scenes by imaging Humbert's obsession with Lolita through two brief shots of her sunglasses (12). The background for Humbert's central action, then, is beautifully established, reverberating throughout the script.

All of this structural complexity plays out in just three pages. Placing the Annabel Leigh adolescent memory between the initial Coalmont sequence and the Ramsdale sequence suggests, as the audience searches for connections, that the traumatic end of an adolescent love through early death has led Humbert, somehow, both to Ramsdale and to Coalmont. Like Nabokov's readers, at first puzzled, the audience seeks interpretive clues.

Pinter soon provides the first one, as we watch Humbert come to the point of rejecting lodgings at Charlotte's, only to change his mind when he sees Lolita in those dark glasses. Shot directions emphasize them a second time as the screenwriter details a series of images from Humbert's point of view: "Her honey-hued shoulders. Her silky, supple bare back. Her stomach. Her dark glasses" (11–12). The filmic or imagistic echo implicitly suggests Humbert's understanding, or rationalization, that his obsession with Lolita and other young girls has been "fated" by his early trauma, and does that much more subtly and with more evocative imagery about ways of "seeing" than does the Schiff and Mamet emphasis on the red beach ball from the same adolescent scene; bewilderingly, like Kubrick, Dearden omits the whole Annabel Leigh sequence.

Another example of Pinter's evocative dexterity in structuring emerges from a brief comparison of Schiff's script with Pinter's skillful treatment of the end of Humbert's first extended, cross-continental trip with Lolita and their settling in Beardsley. Schiff's rendering of the scene in which Lolita finally comments that she is fed up with life on the road is ineffectual, not very rich in suggestion. "How long are we gonna have to live in stuffy cabins doing filthy things and never behaving like ordinary people?" Lolita asks (Schiff, 77). In Pinter's version a similar but expanded, more reverberant, and rhythmically pleasing query clearly leads to Humbert's decision to rent a home and establish domestic life (116). His response, at least in part, springs from his recognition of Lolita's desperate need for something beyond their current parody of a relationship. In Schiff's script, Lolita's complaint leads to Humbert's lecture that they must economize, which reminds Lolita of her mother and makes her cry (77). Through his structuring of the following scenes, Schiff implies that only a combination of Lolita's flirting and Humbert's fear of capture lead him to hurry Lolita back into Beardsley, a less balanced and ambiguous vision than either Pinter's or Nabokov's.

Much of Pinter's pleasing structure results from his felicitous decisions about what to omit from the novel, a reflection of his preferences and talents with exposition. Given the nature of the film medium, a good adaptation usually depends on a relatively straightforward structure. In a well-written novel, we easily understand tangential side roads as structural elements providing parallel comment or context; in a film, such episodes often seem exaggerated digressions. For example, Pinter's script does not include any scenes of Humbert in mental institutions. It also omits the early description of his marriage to Valeria. Humbert tells us in Nabokov's novel that he decided to marry "for my own safety. It occurred to me that regular hours, home-cooked meals, all the conventions of marriage, the prophylactic routine of its bedroom activities, and, who knows, the eventual flowering of certain moral values, of certain spiritual substitutes, might help me, if not to purge myself of my degrading and dangerous desires, at least to keep them under pacific control" (25). He continues that this "piteous compromise" only suggested "how dreadfully stupid poor Humbert was in matters of sex." The horrific marriage ends when a Russian taxi driver steals Humbert's Valeria from beneath his virile nose. Humbert briefly entertains thoughts of murder, but finally regrets not doing anything at all.

In the novel, this episode serves as a foreshadowing parallel of what will happen with Lolita and Humbert, and with Charlotte, with the difference that Humbert takes vengeance on Quilty for violating the "sanctity" of his relationship, ironically for corrupting his rapturous love. Quilty's behavior is a more decadent parallel for what Humbert has already done. In the novel, Humbert's reminiscing about this marriage also parallels his continuing attempts to grow beyond his own depravity.

However, such echoing subplotting is not essential to the main thrust of the narrative, and its omission is all to the good in streamlining the central moral thrust of Humbert's story. By deleting this foreshadowing detail, Pinter also enhances Humbert's mystery for us as the film begins, a typical omission of events from a character's past that characterizes his exposition throughout the work. Similarly, Pinter omits most of the narrative detail in the novel about the sleuthing that Humbert does himself and his hiring of a professional detective to discover Lolita's whereabouts. He omits all of the subplot describing Humbert's affair with Rita as well. In the novel, after Lolita's disappearance, Humbert takes up with this woman of thirty, admittedly of an almost adolescent weight (105 pounds), because of his fear of insanity. The two-year episode has its place in the original, perhaps implying a kind of midstage moral growth for Humbert, but it would distract from the central action in the film.

In addition to his structural acumen, Pinter's inventiveness with Nabokov's rich, often allusive imagery and interior monologue is beautifully apt throughout the script. His skill in the discovery of visual or dialogic equivalents is particularly evident in his sex scenes, which evoke both the horror of Humbert's behavior and simultaneously point toward its similarity to adult romantic love in its wish to control the other as an object. Pinter's sex scenes also suggest, with just the right balance, Lolita's complicity as a willing, even manipulative lover; as with Nabokov's descriptions, they often imply that the sources of her behavior lie in our corrupted culture.

For example, unlike Dearden, Pinter includes a tour-de-force version of the couch masturbation scene. As Charlotte has gone off to church, leaving Lolita behind, the mother has told the daughter "It's your conscience" in the Pinter script (30), which takes as its departure Nabokov's describing Charlotte's going to church without her daughter, who has reneged on the deal to attend services because a promised picnic has been postponed (54). In Pinter's, script, that conscience line reverberates when Lolita asks Humbert during their contest for the red apple which she brings to the game, "What's a conscience? Whatever it is I don't have one" (31). With that we are off and running with Pinter's language for Humbert's distracting dialogue about art, and Michelangelo and Jack

Benny and "Jimmy Schnozzle" Durante and Leonardo da Vinci.

As Humbert tries to keep Lolita on his lap, Pinter's lines succinctly approximate the novel's manic interior monologue, including a portion of Nabokov's allusive "Carmen" song (33–37). Though Humbert sings a supposedly popular song, the Prosper Mérimée tale that Nabokov plays on, the basis for Georges Bizet's opera, tells the story of a treacherous female who takes advantage of a besotted, foolish male. When she takes up with another man and refuses to go with her original paramour, the first man murders her (Proffer, 45–53). Pinter has Humbert sing the song again, very slowly, in a remarkable, invented scene in the desert after he has lost Lolita, underlining his devastation more economically than does Nabokov. Here, the last lyric is about "our final row, / And the gun I killed you with, O my Carmen, / The gun I am holding now" (164).

As in the novel, this misleading foreshadowing intensifies our suspense about whether or not Humbert will actually kill Lolita. In the novel, the attentive reader knows as soon as Lolita's letter comes that he will not, for the preface includes the information that "Mrs. 'Richard Schiller' died in childbirth, giving birth to a stillborn girl, on Christmas Day 1952, in Gray Star, a settlement in the remotest Northwest" (6). Though the Schiller name doesn't crop up until Lolita's letter appears, in the Pinter version the suspense is more emphatic, for we do not have even the preface's revelation. This allows Pinter to keep that element of suspense in the foreground, while still fortuitously omitting Nabokov's most blatant trickery. That occurs in an interior monologue, just after Lolita has told Humbert that she will not go with him: "'It would have made all the difference,' said Humbert Humbert. Then I pulled out my automatic—I mean, this is the kind of a fool thing a reader might suppose I did. It never even occurred to me to do it" (255).

While still emphasizing the horror of the perverse sexuality at its core, this type of subtle labeling of Humbert's intensely sexual story continues to provide a kind of moral construct in Pinter's hands. Just before Humbert goes back to their room at the Enchanted Hunters to consummate his plot to ravish Lolita, Pinter invents a scene where he hears one of Nabokov's clerics speaking on eternity. The comic speech carries an ironic moral label: "All we can say at this stage is that [eternity] goes on for a very very long time indeed. And even then it has hardly begun. So you can all see that it makes a lot of sense to keep on the right side of the Lord" (86). Despite the injunction that he has just heard, Humbert returns to the room, furtively approaching the sleeping Lolita. Here, Pinter amplifies Nabokov's suggestion of the Venetian blinds casting bar-like shadows over Lolita (89). In the Pinter script as Humbert quickly takes off his clothes and slips into his pajamas, Lolita "turns her head and stares—through the striped shadows" (89). The images suggest that she is trapped in a number of ways.

Pinter also includes in excruciating detail the frustrations of Humbert's long night which Nabokov comically recounts. In the script version, a catalogue-like effect takes us to the edge of our seats in suspense. We hear toilets noisily flushing, which we know Humbert fears will wake Lolita from her drugged sleep and foil his plan to work his diseased will on her while she is unconscious. We hear noisy coughing, the clatter of the elevator's descent and its slamming gate, a truck roaring by, the pounding rain and wind shifting those Venetian blinds. Lolita wakes up, tosses, talks in her sleep. Humbert is just about to clutch her to him when mammoth heartburn sets in; belching loudly, he runs for water, and she wakes up once more, demanding her own glass. As the night sounds finally fade, we see Humbert withdraw his hand, thwarted. Then the noises of the awakening hotel begin, the dawn creeping in through those blinds accompanied by another noisy toilet flush (89–92).

As we tend toward an ironic identification with this antihero with whom we have chosen to travel, the often comic Pinter suspense almost allows us to share Humbert's joyful surprise when Lolita begins to fellate him the next morning. *She* suggests that she go down on Humbert in order to better instruct him on the delights that she has learned at her summer camp (93). Two maids, in a vignette typical of Pinter's inventions, remark on how long the couple are lying abed, humorously commenting on a breakfast delivered to the room, "That's some appetite" (94). But, we get at the horror, too, of Humbert's actions, and at more of the cultural backdrop for Lolita's behavior, when Pinter includes a detail from the novel as the two check out the next morning, Lolita seated in a "blood red armchair reading a movie magazine . . . [as] her tongue explores a light rash around her lips" (97). This portrait emphasizes both the adolescence of the youngster whom Humbert has so selfishly possessed, an implied source for her willingness and premature "sophistication," and the atrocious results of his fulfillment.

Most importantly, in this first movement of Humbert's journey with Lolita, Pinter chooses to retain from the novel Humbert's recognition of his moral turpitude as one of his few voice-overs. As Lolita walks toward the car from a gas station rest room, Humbert says, "It was like being with the small ghost of somebody you had recently killed" (100). Pinter's placement of this speech, immediately before Humbert finally gets around to telling Lolita of her mother's death, emphasizes that Humbert has not yet profited from his recognition. Humbert's accepting her coming into his room and his arms, in this context, manages to communicate through filmic image the novel's omitted specific, interior line: "You see, she had absolutely nowhere else to go" (130), which ends "Part I" of the novel at roughly the halfway point. The scene in Pinter's script occurs just past the midway point, as well, broadly faithful to the balance of the novel's structure.

Repeated, brief images of Humbert's taking advantage of Lolita, of her often being bored with his randiness, are still delicately balanced in the Pinter version. Our horror is mitigated by Pinter-invented lines such as Humbert's response to Lolita's accusing him of being a "pervert": "My darling, let me tell you something. A pervert is someone who cannot love. A pervert is someone without a heart. I have a heart and it belongs to you" (108). The line captures both Humbert's self-deception at this stage about the nature of his love and suggests that he does love her on some level, even as he destroys her childhood. Pinter avoids making this dialogue seem ponderous in its signifying with Lolita's adolescent response as she unwraps a stick of gum, "Well gee, thanks. I could really use an extra heart" (109).

Throughout the film, Pinter's sexual imagery is so intense as to invoke very strongly our condemnation of Humbert, but a variety of devices nonetheless allow the audience to develop a sympathy similar to that which the novel encourages. Often that sympathetic element depends on our recognition of Lolita's complicity, of her manipulation of Humbert, and, at least in part, of the sources of her behavior in her culture's emphasis on adolescent sexuality and in her competitive, rebellious relationship with her mother.

One of the most chilling scenes evoking the horror of Humbert's behavior occurs soon after we see Humbert and Charlotte making love. She asks him if he prefers little girls or big girls, as he says that he would like their offspring to be a girl. The camera lingers on his face (47). In the next scene, after reading a letter from Lolita thanking them for the candy and recounting the loss of her sweater in the woods and "having a time," Charlotte rebukes Humbert for sending Lolita candy without consulting her. Ironically, we soon discover that Lolita has abandoned her sweater during an adolescent *ménage à trois*. We cut to Humbert in Lolita's room, with no hesitation going to one of her drawers and taking out an anklet: "he puts the anklet around two fingers and gently draws it tighter." The devastatingly clear suggestion of this Pinter-invented image is that he finds "big girls" too loose, the tight anklet becoming an image of his perverse desire for youthful flesh. The scene is both horrific and titillating, just as it should be in its making our begrudging identification with Humbert a moral exercise in what we should not do or yield to ourselves.

A second, more brutal scene follows Lolita's sending Humbert out from one of their motel rooms for fruit—bananas, as a matter of fact. When he returns, he finds her dressed, her mouth smudged, gravel on her shoes, all economically established. Convinced of her betrayal, "He stares at her, suddenly pushes her back onto the bed, rips her shirt off, unzips her slacks, tears them off. She does not resist. She is naked. She lies still looking up at him. She smiles at him" (146). This scene emphasizes the violence of what Humbert has been doing to Lolita all along, underlining his possessiveness and insecurity. More complexly, it also points to the power of the female object of desire, to her ability to use the situation to manipulate the aggressor, a typical Pinter motif.

In addition to the fellatio scene and her orgasmic response, with an apple, during the couch masturbation scene, several other Pinter scenes forcefully image Lolita's participation or flirtatious encouragement of Humbert's horrific perversion. Early on, we watch Lolita flirt outrageously with Humbert, as she comes into his room, browsing through his books, and finally perching on his knee, examining his doodlings:

LOLITA: What's all this?

HUMBERT: Oh . . . doodling . . . just doodling.

LOLITA: Doodling?

HUMBERT: Yes.

She shifts on his knee. His eyes are half closed.

HUMBERT: Yes.

LOLITA: But I don't know what it's supposed to be. What's it supposed to be?

HUMBERT: Nothing.

She wriggles on his knee.

LOLITA: So you call this doodling?

We get directions for a shot of her parted lips, of her hair; then she asks if she has a pimple on her chin, if Humbert can see it. Shouting out that she needs some "cream," she hops off his knee, running out of the room in the first dress we've seen her wear (24–25). The sexuality of this simple scene, like that of Ruth and her glass of water in *The Homecoming*, fairly boils—and beats Kubrick's having Lolita feed Humbert his bacon by many miles.

A more blatant version of Lolita's manipulation and participation in sexual matters occurs soon after her enrollment at the Beardsley School, where Miss Pratt, with the Reverend Rigger's approval, has espoused the school's guiding principle, the "three D's—Dramatics, Dance and Dating" (119). As Lolita pleads with Humbert to allow her to participate in a school play, she "dances over to him, sinking to the floor by his knees. She rests her head on his knee. She puts her hand on the inside of his knee. He continues reading. Her hand gently creeps a little way up his inner thigh" (121).

Her hand goes higher, he closes his eyes, and she demands a doubling of her allowance. When he resists, her hand retreats; she reiterates her request, now asking that she be allowed to act in the play. Her hand begins to climb his thigh again (122). Then we cut to a scene of Humbert making the bed, examining the sheet, turning it over and tucking it in, only to be interrupted by the housekeeper. Echoing the tone of Pinter's early one-act play, *The Lover* (1963), the scene should allow the audience to make interpretive connections easily, recognizing that this apparently pathological sexuality is similar to the manipulative quality of the "straight" adult variety. Pinter lowers the mounting tension nicely, but then raises it as we watch Humbert's fear of discovery in his own home, a horrifying way to live.

After Lolita's matriculation at the ridiculous Beardsley School, we continue to condemn Humbert for his obsessive and destructive sexual behavior, but we also tend toward greater sympathy for him as he overtly plays the role of the protective parent of a daughter whom he sees as endangered by an impoverished society, its authority figures who supposedly guide the young, and her pathetically shallow peers. Although Pinter includes both horrific and comic examples of Humbert's pedophilia, our knowledge that Quilty is hovering about, a new threat to Lolita, coupled with scenes showing Humbert trying to do his best by her are powerful balancing elements. For example, one morning we see Humbert bearing an enormous breakfast in celebration of Lolita's fourteenth birthday.

Before he will let her eat a bite, he takes her downstairs to see her brand new bicycle. She's wonderfully excited, flinging her arms around him and calling him "Dad" in a genuinely touching scene (127–28). A Pinter invention, this unmediated dramatic scene springs from Humbert's brief mention of the present in the novel ("For her birthday I bought her a bicycle," 182) and from his earlier description of watching Lolita's grace in riding her "beautiful young bicycle" (171). That earlier scene includes another of Nabokov's images of rapture, which Pinter allows Humbert after the party in his version, once more in slow motion (132), as in his rendering of the tennis scene.

That party, which Humbert permits Lolita to attend to aid her "normal development," includes inventive Pinter dialogue that unobtrusively points in thematic directions. After the young people discuss Quilty as being "pretty old" or "not that old," we hear a parody of a discussion of God. As the conversations continue in counterpoint, with Jim asking Lolita about Quilty, Mona asks Roy what he thinks about predestination. He replies, "I think it stinks. I mean if you don't have free will—who needs it?" (131). The "dramatic" scene evokes the Nabokov ideas about fate versus free will, which the novelist voices through Humbert's contemplative interior monologues. The hint from which Pinter's filmic version springs is Humbert's very brief mention in the novel that the young people were discussing "Predestination and the law of averages" (182). In Pinter's scene, with Humbert's intrusive entrance on the youngster's party in search of lemonade, the effect of the expanded predestination comments is to label Humbert an exemplum of free will gone awry, a man who has constantly tried to blame fate or youthful fixation for his life. He is much like another Pinter film character, Leo in *The Go-Between*, who destroys his life for much the same reasons.

This mixed tone, fruitful, ironic ambiguity, continues as Lolita successfully manages her plot to leave town, with her picking the spots where they will rendezvous with Quilty. Unaware of being duped, Humbert is overjoyed when they arrive at home after her running away and after her mysterious phone call, which *we* know is to Quilty; she peels off her sweater, saying "Carry me upstairs. I feel sort of romantic tonight" (140). The shot of Lolita, holding out her arms, naked once that sweater is off, is evocative, echoing the lost sweater in the woods of long ago, and just right. She is excited about her new plot, and she is going to take it out on Humbert. The attempt at grown-up sophistication, awkward though it is in Lolita's mouth, perfectly images the complexity of emotions percolating in Lolita far too early, unfortunately characteristic of far too many children in our "real" world.

As Humbert becomes Quilty's and Lolita's victim, our begrudging sympathy for him continues. Those enigmatic, threatening cars are in pursuit by this point (146), his suspicions about Lolita's betraying him growing to a fever pitch. We are still not allowed to forget what Humbert has done to Lolita, though. Just as she is about to leave Humbert, Pinter includes Nabokov's image of the mannequins in the dress shop window—a device similar to Pinter's and Ian McEwan's in *The Comfort of Strangers* where the young British couple contemplates two mannequins reclined on a coldly futuristic bed in a Venice store window (12–13, 21 in the novella). Here, our odd couple looks at the naked models in the window, one wigless and armless, the other a bride with just one arm, limbs on the floor, twisted (151). The figures carry clear imagistic weight for what Humbert has done to Lolita, as, similarly warped, she prepares to leave him, talking to a bald man in an oatmeal coat from the red convertible very soon after (152).

Pinter's marvelous version of Humbert's rapture over Lolita's performance at tennis—"her volleys and her service possess infinite grace, harmony, lightness and charm"—calls for the scene to be shot in slow motion (156). The slow motion emphasizes that we see Lolita from Humbert's point of view for the moment, an emphatic contrast to Quilty's joking, clowning response to Lolita's tennis. Quilty, during the time that Humbert has gone to answer a sham phone call, "slaps Lolita on her bottom with his racquet. He suddenly sees Humbert, drops his racquet and scuttles into the shrubbery, waving his wrists and elbows as if flying" (158).

Pinter softens our response to Humbert slightly, too, by omitting the horrific scene in the novel where Humbert lusts after Lolita during the fever that precedes her being hospitalized. Nabokov has Humbert meditate on her illness in perhaps the most sexual terms in the novel:

> Her skin was scalding hot! . . . Hysterical little nymphs might, I knew, run up all kinds of temperature—even exceeding a fatal count. And I would have given her a sip of hot spiced wine, and two aspirins, and kissed the fever away, if, upon an examination of her lovely uvula, one of the gems of her body, I had not seen that it was a burning red. I undressed her. Her breath was bittersweet. Her brown rose tasted of blood. She was shaking from head to toe. . . . Giving up all hope of intercourse, I wrapped her up in a laprobe and carried her into the car. (219)

Pinter's substituting a scene with a receptionist at the motel insisting on taking Lolita's temperature (160) makes for a much more sympathetic Humbert than the original, sick, obsessive portrait rendered by Nabokov. Thus, Humbert's gentle caring at the hospital and his impassioned response when he discovers the ruse whereby Lolita has been whisked away emerge more clearly both as evidence of his love, and of his possessiveness, and of his obsession, a complex mix (163). Consistent with this ambiguously sympathetic understanding, the aftermath of her flight provides us with a label of sorts as Pinter describes Humbert's tearing up Lolita's movie magazines but gently folding and putting away her clothes (165). It is as if he is kept the best of Lolita and is throwing away the worst, that which has conditioned her depravity, which, in turn, has allowed him to succeed in his lustful goals.

After Lolita's letter drops into the box under the caption "Three Years Later," we return to the beginning scene of the film, with a few shots repeated, including that with the gun and the reverently handled bobby pin (165–67). Pinter has prepared us, subtly and ambiguously, to recognize Humbert's growth in his scene with Lolita Schiller, which is very faithful to the novel. He chooses not to use in voice-over Humbert's interior monologue about not just adoring the nymph but loving the mature Lolita:

> and I looked and looked at her, and knew as clearly as I know I am to die that I loved her more than anything I had ever seen or imagined on earth, or hoped for anywhere else. She was only the faint violet whiff and dead leaf echo of the nymphet I had rolled myself upon with such cries in the past; . . . [B]ut thank God it was not that echo alone that I worshipped . . . [my] sterile and selfish vice, all that I canceled and cursed. . . . I insist that the world know how much I loved my Lolita, this Lolita, pale and polluted, and big with another man's child. (253)

But Pinter's clear dialogue and imagery, Humbert's despair at his recognition that Lolita will not come with him, is enough to make the point. Pinter does include Nabokov's line where she calls him "honey" as she rejects him, "No honey, no" (175). In the novel, Humbert muses to himself, "she'd never called me honey before" (254), suggesting that she recognizes a change in Humbert or that Humbert ardently wishes for even this level of affection. Pinter achieves much the same effect by having Humbert pause a moment and ask, "Did you call me honey?" (174).

Pinter also softens our potentially harsh judgement of Humbert in the scene where he murders Quilty. The screenwriter omits Nabokov's ambiguous poem/indictment that Humbert forces Quilty to read, which underlines Humbert's own guilt and jealousy. The original poem also includes the evocative accusation that Quilty has cheated Humbert of his "redemption" (273–74). Still, leaving out the poem allows Pinter to highlight the fact that Humbert twice claims to be Lolita's father in the "prose" indictment that remains, yet here he calls her only Dolores Haze, or Dolly Haze, never the Lolita of the beginning obsessive speech, the "she was always Lolita in my arms" lines. So, given what Lolita has told us of her life with Quilty, who has stolen her on a lark to share with others, we again tend toward sympathizing, perhaps even admiring Humbert in his final mission. That is particularly so as we see Quilty's guests revel in their decadence and say that someone should have killed him long ago, and as two young girls smile at Humbert, who leaves them behind without a second glance, his obsessive pedophilia vanquished (186–87).

Pinter's finale resonates as Nabokov's novel does with that image of the children down in the valley. More evocative than Dearden's truncated version and more concise than Schiff's, Pinter's direction reads: "A growing sound from the valley. The sound consists of a melody of children at play. It is distant. It vibrates, murmurs, sings. Humbert stands still." The last line suggests contemplation, and then, in voice-over once more, Humbert whispers, "light of my life, fire of my loins. My sin, my soul. Lo—lee—ta" (188).

That contemplation, that juxtaposition of sin and soul, points us toward both major elements of the mystery that is finally Nabokov's Humbert—but with the subtle, cumulative suggestion that he has come to a profound recognition that he has wronged Lolita by robbing her of her childhood. That selfish theft has occurred, in part because of his own loss of childhood, of both mother and first love, *and* because of his inability to overcome, through strength of will, that traumatic experience for many years. The terrible irony, of course, is that Pinter's two captions, like Nabokov's introduction, reveal that both characters die soon after their mutual progress toward a new kind of moral maturity:

HUMBERT DIED OF A CORONARY
THROMBOSIS ON NOVEMBER 16, 1952.

LOLITA DIED IN CHILDBIRTH ON
CHRISTMAS DAY 1952.

That Lolita dies in childbirth on Christmas Day, and that her child is stillborn, embodies one of the darkest ironies of the novel. Yet, we admire her all the more because of her ability to choose "the good" at the end of her life, despite a painfully disturbing youth, which, after all, was similar to Humbert's. She has managed to overcome such horrific loss and impoverishment more quickly than her admirer, but with perhaps less insight.

The audience's insights into Humbert, though, are at the crux of this novel, and central to the evaluation of any successful adaptation. Richard Corliss quotes Kubrick as saying:

> Naturally I regret that the film could not be more erotic. . . . The eroticism of the story served a very important purpose in the book: it obscured any hint that Humbert loved Lolita. . . . It was very important to delay an awareness of his love until the end of the story. I'm afraid that this was all too obvious in the film. But in my view this is the only justifiable criticism. (85)

Corliss concludes that the criticism is a central one, since "Moviegoers are denied the therapeutic revelation that a monster can be sanctified" (85). Though "sanctified" goes too far, unlike the Pinter script, the three other *Lolita* screenplays from the nineties all compromise that "therapeutic revelation" in one way or another. Dearden's script, particularly in the writer's choosing to omit the Annabel Leigh allusions in Humbert's memories of his first tryst, is at best pedestrian, often wrongheaded in its tone, and awkward in its dialogue. For just one example, in that central scene where Humbert briefly reunites with the pregnant Lolita, instead of the novel's emphasis on her moral growth in her refusal to speak of sexual degradation with the baby in the womb, Dearden has her say his invented, unbearably corny line: "Whoosh! He's gonna play for the Giants, for sure" (130).

Mamet's dialogue is certainly more skilled and evocative, but Mamet's script is the least faithful to the spirit of the novel as I understand it. By omitting the novel's scenes depicting Humbert's renting a home in Beardsley and eliding the two journeys, Mamet makes Humbert a much more one-sided villain. The screenwriter also invents several lines that point to Humbert's mere weak-willed culpability, as in Humbert's reply to Charlotte's question, "Do you think, darling, that we search for excuses to do that which we were going to do in any case?" Humbert responds, "Yes.

They call it weakness" (63). Particularly since Mamet leaves out the novel's emphasis on Annabel Leigh's and Humbert's mother's deaths, Humbert emerges as only a mad, negative example. With his decision also to omit the aftermath of Quilty's murder, particularly Humbert's hearing the sound of those children as emblems for his recognition of his culpability, Mamet's conclusion in another mental institution makes Humbert unambiguous, a character not so suggestive as he is in the novel and in the Pinter filmscript.

The shooting script by Schiff displays a critical intelligence. Still, this is a script by committee, in effect, for it seemingly includes elements of all three of the earlier scripts. The forcefulness of a personal vision of the spirit of the novel is decimated.[3] As Lyne suggested, the humor and the sex scenes are indeed "punched up" (Brennan, F14), but too far in my judgment, and, as he early on suggested to Pinter, the shooting script relies heavily on voice-over.

The Pinter version is much truer to the spirit of the novel, while still taking advantage of the different potentials of the film medium. The author's limited use of well chosen voice-overs and the visualized dramatic scenes that take the place of many of Humbert's musings on his own behavior work beautifully. The essential problem in this adaptation is threefold: (1) to render the moral horror of Humbert's behavior, which should carry metaphoric weight beyond his obsession with nymphets; (2) to show, at the same time, Humbert's own rationalization of his behavior; (3) to paint a portrait of romantic love, even rapture—all the while leaving open the possibility of our recognition of Humbert's moral growth. Pinter's adaptation emphasizes the dramatic action of the novel in total, the human events that are really at its core. He manages to include all three of these arenas more successfully than do the other scripts.

At its core, Pinter's adaptation is so successful because his ear for language results in an intelligent echoing and fruitful reshaping of Nabokov's descriptions of Humbert's interior musings and memories, and because his restructuring of the novel so aptly fits it to the film medium. Pinter's finding filmic or dialogue equivalents for Humbert's voice is often wondrous, as in his language for Humbert's flight of fancy during the couch masturbation scene, or in his rendering of Humbert's suspenseful frustration during his long night at that first hotel, or in his minimal but reverberant lines from Humbert's father about Annabel's death. Furthermore, Pinter's invention of new dialogue that reflects the spirit of the novel is equally adept, providing fruitfully ambiguous moral labels, such as included in the minister's comments at the Enchanted Hunters, the maids' conversation outside Humbert's and Lolita's motel room, and the adolescents' conversation about predestination in the Beardsley party scene.

The rigorous, intelligent structure of Pinter's script is the most impressive element of this difficult adaptation. As we have seen, Pinter's decision to begin at Coalmont, as Humbert approaches Lolita's down-and-out marital abode, gun in pocket, allows the writer to focus our attention, right from the start, on the moral crux of the novel. In effect, Pinter begins *in medias res*, providing "exposition" through Humbert's musings over his past (which is so much a part of his present), allowing us to see Humbert's revision of himself through his actions. That skilled structuring also depends on Pinter's honing of the work, on his reducing it to its essential action by omitting Nabokov's scenes of Humbert's marriage to Valeria, of his residing in mental institutions, of his detective work after Lolita's disappearance, and of his affair with the thirty-year-old Rita. Unerringly centering on what is best about the novel, and most essential, Pinter's structure allows a blending of both sympathy and condemnation of Humbert and Lolita, and the recognition of their moral growth.

Typically, in Pinter's work, actions speak much more emphatically than either words or silences. With a grim irony, he shows Humbert's conversion coming too late, though its evidence is moving, in his newly realized love for Lolita, in his recognition of the horrific, destructive behavior of his past, and in his overcoming his pedophilia. Like Oedipus, Humbert's courage at facing and recognizing his own flaw, his recognition that he has conditioned his fatedness, is his nobility. Unfortunately, that courage comes far too late in the game, as forcefully suggested in Pinter's script, to undo the damage he has already wrought. Still, as in Pinter's plays, the portrait of love in Nabokov's novel, even when enraptured, emerges most often as a matter of control, of possession of an object, or of being possessed—emphatically not a mutual, free sharing between equal adults. In Pinter's *Lolita,* we are confronted with images that encourage a similar recognition and ask us to go beyond such behavior, as Humbert finally does in his love for the mature Delores Haze.

NOTES

1. Harold Pinter has been wonderfully generous to me over the last fifteen or sixteen years, graciously offering help and encouragement. I thank him now

and again for his many kindnesses. I thank David Mamet, as well, for his generosity in sending me a copy of his *Lolita*. Thanks, also, to Zoran Kuzmanovich, the president of the Nabokov Society, for sending me a copy of his MLA paper, to the staff of the Margaret Herrick Library of the American Academy of Motion Picture Arts and Sciences in Los Angeles, and to the University of Nevada, Las Vegas, for funding both my London and Los Angeles research trips.

2. Much of the original film's imbalance or comic excess, I think, indirectly results from Kubrick's frustration at not being able to work explicitly with the novel's sexual themes in 1962. While Nabokov finally yielded to Kubrick's request that he write a screenplay, Kubrick and his colleagues, including Peter Sellers, rewrote the script. Producer James B. Harris and Kubrick told Nabokov that it was "the best screenplay ever written in Hollywood." Yet in 1993, Harris said of Nabokov's lengthy script: "You couldn't make it. You couldn't *lift* it." Despite Nabokov's screenplay credit, he rewrote his script and published it as *Lolita: A Screenplay* (New York: McGraw Hill, 1974). See Corliss (16, 19).

3. In Pinter's letter to me of November 21, 1995, he comments, interestingly, "I didn't read the Dearden script." He also remarks that he has "never read the Edward Albee play," to my mind a very strange and unsuccessful dramatic adaptation.

CHAPTER TEN

⊞

Isak Dinesen with a Contemporary Social Conscience: Harold Pinter's Film Adaptation of "The Dreaming Child"

FRANCIS X. GILLEN

Isak Dinesen's "The Dreaming Child" is read by most critics of her work as an expression of her artistic belief in the aristocratic superiority of the imagined world to the world of mere fact. Through the transforming power of the child from the slums that Emilie Vandamm and her husband Jakob bring into their house, Emilie moves from what Dinesen terms "a creed of fanatical truthfulness and solidity" (162) to an existential reconciliation of such apparently logical opposites as truth and falsity.

It is easy to see the resonances which Dinesen's tale must have struck within Harold Pinter's own imagination at the time he began work on this 1997 screenplay. Though set in an earlier time period, here in the tale are the two worlds of secure privilege and need seen in both the screen and television versions of *Party Time* and the imaginative empathy which allows Rebecca in *Ashes to Ashes* to bridge gaps of time, space, and identity to feel the pain of a Holocaust victim and relate it to her own need to be free of a self-imposed victimization.

Dinesen's tale begins with an extended history of the Plejelt family. She notes their weaknesses and failings and an old judge's surmise that if they don't pull themselves together, "the rats will eat them" (154). While most of the clan thereafter unexpectedly thrived, one unfortunate girl seemed to pull down upon herself the family's ill fate. She died in childbirth before she was twenty, leaving Madame Mahler $106 to provide for the child, a sum provided by the unknown father, who, the narrator tells us, "is otherwise unknown to this tale" (154).

As the boy, Jens, grows up in the slums of Copenhagen, he begins to feel that he does not belong in such squalor, a sentiment reinforced by a new occupant of the house, Mamzell Ane, a seamstress who lives secure in her memories of the grand houses in which she had worked and the aristocratic ways and deeds of their inhabitants. She dreams of a revolutionary future in which no one will be deprived of "those highest human values" of "grandeur, beauty and elegance" (157). In his turn, Jens begins to tell the impoverished children with whom he plays of his wealthy mother and father and their grand world which is his true home. Before she dies when Jens is but six, Mamzell Ane assures the boy that it is not uncommon for a boy of such circumstances to be suddenly lost from his true parents.

Dinesen's tale then shifts to the Vandamms, a wealthy, childless couple who had been engaged since childhood. At eighteen, while Jakob had been away, Emilie had fallen in love with a naval officer, Charlie Dreyer. Pressed by the passionate Charlie to allow him to spend the night before his departure, Emilie had wavered but refused his passion and had closed the gate of her family home against him. Shortly thereafter, she received news of Charlie's death. By the age of twenty she has married Jakob, is mistress of her house, and has more or less settled for a life devoid of passion but dedicated to stolidity and works of "proper" charity, which clearly distinguish between the "deserving and undeserving" poor.

As their marriage continues and they have no children, the question of an heir arises. Driving through the slum, Jakob encounters Jens, knocking him down as the boy stands unmoving in front of his horse. After negotiations with Madame Mahler, Emilie brings Jens into her home for a six-month trial period. As she sees the impoverished children of the slum, she feels for the first time "personally related to the need and misery of the world" (168). Jens simply accepts his entrance into the splendor of the Vandamm household as an exile's return to his rightful home and family. With the power of a "dreamer whose dreams come true"

(171), he transforms its inhabitants by becoming the mirror of an ideal that they are impelled to live. Unfortunately, Emilie cannot love him.

The essence of the boy, however, is a longing that moves him ineffably away from the situation in which he finds himself and toward its shadow. Safely ensconced in an ideal world, his imagination moves back to his other world where there are dark, dirt, rats, and people so poor that they had to sleep standing up with a rope for support. Like a young tree that dies early because it has shot out a profusion of flowers without taking deep root, Jens begins to decline. As Emilie attends his sickbed, she ponders her own attempt to separate life into easy categories of good and bad and reflects on the diminutive Jens as one "to whom these were all one, who welcomed light and darkness, pleasure and pain, in the same spirit of gallant, debonair approval and fellowship" (178).

After Jens' death, Emilie seems to decline until a day several months later when Jakob takes her into the countryside and they walk in the woods. Jens, she tells Jakob, was her child and Charlie Dreyer's, and she asks him to understand that Charlie's desire for her had come from his love and his great heart. Whereas before she knew Jens, she believed that she must suffer for this, now she believes in a world beyond categories, for "There is a grace in the world, such as none of us has known about. The world is not a hard or severe place as people tell us. It is not even just. You are forgiven everything. The fine things of the world you cannot wrong or harm; they are much too strong for that" (187). Things would be easier for both of them, she tells Jakob, if he would believe her, and he responds with some ambiguity, "'Yes, my dear, . . . that is true'" (188).

Dinesen's tale, like many of her works, reflects her view that the only way to escape life's often painful contradictions is to accept and embrace them. Her model for Emilie may have been her grandmother, Mary Hansen, for whom a spark of passion had been ignited by her music teacher. According to one of Dinesen's biographers, Judith Thurman, after Mary's father suppressed the relationship with some brutality, Mary acquired an "overdeveloped" sense of good and evil, a belief that her judgments on such matters, especially those of a sexual nature, were irrefutable, which she imposed on her children and grandchildren (9).

As she writes in *Shadows on the Grass*, unlike her grandmother, Dinesen believes that in art and dream we have "forsaken our allegiance to the organizing, controlling, and rectifying forces of the world, the universal Conscience. We have sworn fealty to the wild, incalculable, creative forces, the Imagination of the universe" (Hannah, 104). For Robert Langbaum, imagination in the story "unites not only nature and civilization, but also that social spectrum which is one of the subjects of *Winter's Tales*" (171). He also calls attention to the tale's mythic dimensions: the deliverance of the lost child from the cyclops-like, one-eyed Madame Mahler; the biblical Joseph who rules Egypt because, like Jens, his dreams came true; the Divine Child, usually a foundling among humble people, who has magical powers (173).

In denying and suppressing her own deepest feelings, Emilie had become estranged from nature, love, and others and is delivered from that alienation by the power of Jens, who possesses the simplicity of nature in its acceptance of dark and light, life and death. In the final scene, Emilie is able to recover her childhood and repair in a unifying vision the effects of a fall that for Dinesen, as for the poet William Blake, is seen in terms of a division into opposites. As Donald Hannah observes, "For her [Dinesen], art and dreams possess a truth of their own, offer a freedom from moral imperatives and a release from actuality by creating a realm in which the truth of the imagination becomes the supreme reality" (164).

Dinesen is essentially a spinner of leisurely told tales in which the narrative voice is dominant. In creating the screenplay of one of her tales, therefore, a screenwriter must invent some of the dialogue that is left unspoken in the text. Dinesen simply tells us, for example, that as Jens moved into the house of Jakob and Emilie, he "took possession of the mansion in Bredgade, and brought it into submission, neither by might nor by power, but in the quality of that fascinating and irresistible personage, perhaps the most fascinating and irresistible in the world: the dreamer whose dreams come true" (171). In emphasizing the power of such an artist/dreamer, Dinesen tells the reader that the inhabitants of that house then "were made to see themselves with the eyes of the dreamer, and were impelled to live up to an idea" (172). Part of Pinter's difficult task was to find visual metaphors for this spell and to add dialogue to accompany them. As he creates these and other scenes, Pinter does so in keeping with an overall conception of the tale that emphasizes the social more than the theme of the artist. There is, after all, a certain sentimentality in Dinesen's work. Jens is rescued from the slum and poverty, but much as with Charles Dickens's *Oliver Twist*, the uneasy question remains: What of the other children not fortunate enough to have a wealthy relative or, in this case, to have been run into by Jakob's horse?

Through the scenes that he adds, Pinter's acute social conscience deconstructs Dinesen's story by clarifying the reality beyond this single instance of rescue. He broadens the meaning of Emilie's repressed sexuality, making it a metaphor for all that is repressed by Victorian society or, indeed, by any society in the name of maintaining its self-assured, sanctimonious order.

In the opening scenes of the screenplay, Pinter employs the cinematic device of cutting swiftly back and forth from the world of privilege and repression to the world of poverty and degradation. The sordid birth of Jens (Jack in Pinter's script)[1] and his mother's death is interposed with scenes of Emilie's (Emily) rejection of Charlie (Charley), light and brilliant sunlight or moonlight cuts to death and darkness, slumhouse to mansion, garden or a grand ball. Similarly, the wedding of Tom (Jakob) and Emily is interspersed with swift cuts of Charley's funeral. At the wedding Emily's face is "impassive."

The scene then shifts to Jack's life in the slum when he is seven: voices screaming obscenities, broken windows, whistling wind, rats, Jack caught in the flapping sheets of the washing by which Madame Mahler (Mrs. Jones) earns a meager living and then being teased for "thinking."

Again cutting back to the mansion, Pinter creates three characters: Emily's friend Peggy, her husband Rupert, and a vicar. As they talk in the billiard room, they discuss votes for women, which the vicar calls "unnatural, ungodly, and corrupt." We see Emily in control as she plays perfectly but, as at her wedding, without emotion. After the introduction of Mamzell Ane (Miss Scott), the theme of religious suppression and hypocrisy is reinforced as the children teasing Jack are seen carrying Bibles. The dialogue is pure Pinter:

BOY 1: What's this book?

BOY 3: He can't read.

BOY 2: He left his brains in the bog.

BOY 1: This is a Bible. It's all about God.

GIRL: And Jesus.

BOY 3: Jesus wouldn't have anything to do with him.

BOY 2: Nor wouldn't God.

GIRL: Yes, he would. God loves everyone.

BOY 3 (*to Jack*): Get down on your knees then.

(He pushes Jack)

Get down on your knees and pray to God. Pray to God! Pray to God!

ALL THE BOYS (*jostling Jack*): Pray to God! Pray to God! Pray to God!

> (*Jack hits Boy 3 in the face. The boys retreat. Boy 3 starts to cry, holding his face.*)

BOY 1 (*to Jack*): Leave my brother alone. Bastard! We've all got brothers and sisters here. You've got nothing.

Religious suppression becomes general sexual repression in the next scene, as we see Tom entering a whorehouse and leaving angrily, mocked for being shy. Though there is mention in Dinesen's tale of Tom having been with whores before marriage, Pinter changes the emphasis somewhat by placing the scene after Tom's marriage, thus suggesting that Emily's unacknowledged sexual desire for Charley has led to something less than a sexually fulfilling marriage. Later, we see Emily wincing as she and Tom make love.

Then, in a series of scenes in which Miss Scott shares with Jack, her vision of the grander, more aristocratic life she had known in the houses where she had worked, Pinter also adds social details. Miss Scott was simply dismissed when she was deemed too old. When an innocent Jack asks why there are not beautiful houses for all, the screenwriter reinforces Dinesen's suggestion that Mamzell Ane was something of a revolutionary by having her affirm:

MISS SCOTT: There should be. There will be, one day. One day the tables will be turned.

JACK: The tables?

MISS SCOTT: One day the tables will be turned.

Eventually, as in the Dinesen version, she convinces Jack that he does not belong here and that he has been "lost" by his true parents. In the meantime, Pinter dramatizes Emily performing the works of charity expected of a Victorian woman. He shows, as George Bernard Shaw does in *Major Barbara*, poor people reciting the "appropriate" words deemed necessary to receive Christian help, as well as Emily's quickness and certainty in judging a man unworthy of such help because she notices a bottle of beer on the windowsill. When Tom tells her that she is very strict for refusing to aid this man's family because she considers him a drunk, Emily responds, "I am rational." Immediately, Pinter cuts to a scene that he added which shows the luxury that she and her class simply take for granted: she is discussing with the cook and butler the ordinary dinner planned which includes bisque of oysters, whitebait, fillets of salmon, cutlets of pigeon, saddle of mutton, roast quails with watercress, and vanilla mousse.

From the presentation of such luxury, there is a quick cut to Jack in the privy as a rat races along the ground and a drunk threatens to drown Jack in offal. Pinter then returns to the estate, introducing a character, the sixteen-year-old maid Bess, whom the screenwriter has also created. As Bess relays the information that there is no cure for her ailing mother, Emily tells her to have faith, a line that she seems to recite by heart. Such discussion of the poor as seen from above continues in the next scene as Tom and Emily talk with Uncle Edward, Sir George, and Lady Downing (additional characters created by Pinter), with Uncle Edward expressing the seemingly Calvinistic view that the poor are doomed "to eternal degradation." When the word "eternal" seems too much, Edward explains that such earthly degradation "feels likes eternity." Crossly, Lady Downing claims that the filthy poor would not know what to do with water if it were given to them. Emily asserts the need for "detachment" and "hard-headedness" in dispensing charitable funds, and Edward expresses the sentiment taken from Dinesen's text that he finds "the contrast between the suppleness of your [Emily's] body and the rigidity of your mind piquant."

Pinter then recounts the events leading up to Jack's rescue from poverty, following his source rather closely: Miss Scott's death, the need for an heir as Tom and Emily come to believe that they cannot have children, Tom's horse running into Jack in the slum, the agreement to bring the child on a six-month trial basis, and Emily's solitary journey to bring home the child. As in the tale, Jack immediately claims to recognize his mother and to know the horse and the household.

Pinter does add a few scenes that emphasize the social themes of repression and lack of empathy. Tom visits a whore to be assured that he is a "right-ram" and that presumably any infertility is not his fault. When the whore dares mention his wife, however, he slaps her for her impudence in speaking freely of her betters. Emily, in turn, is absolved by her friend and confidante Peggy, who tells her that the only possible reason for infertility is a woman's betrayal of her husband. Finally, as Emily drives toward the mansion with Jack, Pinter has her thinking of Charley, leading him through the house toward her bedroom. This scene is done in sepia, as are all the scenes that occur only in Emily's frustrated desire.

It is in the scenes which follow, as Jack takes possession of the house, that the social emphasis of Pinter's adaptation becomes most apparent. For Dinesen, the events represent the complete, if momentary, triumph of the dreamer. All of the members of the household become part of Jack's aristocratic dream, and with the exception of Emily, they feel themselves pulled by destiny into a more grand conception of themselves, losing even their individuality as they fall under the spell of the artist whose dream has become a reality.

In Pinter's script we are made aware of Jack's power as he feels totally at ease with all parts of the household. Almost immediately, however, Jack is awakened screaming from a dream in which he sees a rat. We see Emily and Tom lying in bed with their eyes open. The power that Jack exerts in the film is an almost egalitarian one. We see him ignoring the class structure in his innocent acceptance of all persons: washing plates in the kitchen, playing jokes with the servants, throwing apples down to the servants in an orchard, and standing on a ladder cleaning candles on the chandelier. We see him developing an affection for the young maid, Bess, and going innocently to her room where he finds a warmth that he does not feel with Emily. Bess, after all, has just lost her mother and for a moment these are just two children together:

> BESS: This is my bed. Look. Do you like my doll? My mum made it all by herself. She gave it to me. She's dead now. She died only the other day, my mum. (She kisses the doll.) I love my doll.

However, Pinter constantly contrasts such scenes with other scenes which reassert the class structures so that there is never the complete triumph of the dreamer as there is in Dinesen's tale. Jack is reprimanded by both the cook and Emily for washing dishes because that is maid's work. The scene in the orchard is followed by one in which Mr. Rudd, Emily's father, calls Jack a savage and claims that he will inherit the immorality of his mother and thus be unworthy of the proposed inheritance. The scene with the servants and Jack cleaning the chandelier ends abruptly as Tom and Emily return. Most significant, though, is the cruel, cold dismissal of Bess. The housekeeper had seen Jack in her room and as Jack is playing one morning, we see the sobbing Bess being led away and then Jack standing in Bess's empty room.

At the same time, we see Emily also going back and forth between her rigidity of mind and a more open attitude. She defends Jack against her father's attack, reminding her father that, if Jack is a child of the poor, he is also not "a thing," only later to slap Jack when she sees him swinging on the very gate that she had shut against Charley. Clearly, she has begun to identify Charley and Jack. She is also spontaneous with Jack at a fairground as she throws a ball and wins a prize. Yet, she confesses to Peggy that she cannot love Jack: "I think I have a desert where my heart should be. An empty space." This conversation is interrupted by her repressed vision of Charley making love to her, her inability to love Tom now clearly linked with her fear of acknowledging what she still believes to be a forbidden love.

The logic of a world order versus the intuition of its essence is then suggested by a scene in which Jack corrects his tutor. India, Jack claims, is "round the corner." When the tutor complains that there are no corners in a globe, Jack admits the teacher's logical correctness, but insists, "I say things that I don't understand. I hear myself say something I don't understand." In this and other scenes in the shipyard when distant places are discussed, Jack shows his sense of the interconnectedness of all things.

In Dinesen's tale, Jack's illness is attributed to everything he dreamed having been fulfilled. For Dinesen, as we have seen, the boy is like a plant that flowers brilliantly before it has had the opportunity to take deep root and so must die. Pinter has Jack's vision of belonging directly contradicted by a girl at a children's party who tells him that he was found in a slum and that he is not Jack or Emily's real child. After that we see more frequent scenes of Jack climbing the stairs to the servants' quarters, looking into Bess's room. As if Jack could suddenly sense the emptiness beneath all the apparent splendor, the pain which in his innocent empathy with the servants he has felt, he now takes ill. As he does so, Jack begins to talk about his old habitation: "Oh, yes, this is a beautiful house. But I have another house. A dark house. A house of dirt and rats."

Once again, as with the tutor, logic will not work. Jack is dying. But of what? Only on a level of intuitive empathy can that question be answered, and for the remainder of the script, Pinter demonstrates Emily's journey toward that identification. First, Jack asks for the scissors that Miss Scott had left him. He wants to cut a white rose from the bush, but Emily had not allowed white roses in her house for they are associated with Charlie. Now, however, Emily makes the journey to the slum to get the scissors for Jack. When Mrs. Jones says Jack was only dreaming, Emily goes to a haberdasher to buy a pair of scissors, presumably willing to break social convention and lie to Jack. At the haberdasher's, she sees a suffragette speech and notices the dismissed Bess among the group. Then, when Emily and Jack are alone, Jack enters into her forbidden dream.

> JACK: Yes. And when you were standing with my father at the gate in the moonlight you plucked a white rose from the bush and you gave it to him.

Finally, before Jack's death, Pinter creates an effective scene in which the dichotomy between the two worlds is apparent:

> JACK: Do you know. . . . I sometimes wonder where I am. I sometimes wonder who I was.
> EMILY: Ssshh. Ssshh.
> JACK: Who was I?

After his death, Jack's effect is shown on Emily's father who now recommends that he be buried in the family vault. As the boy's coffin goes into the vault, we see the iron gates close, as they had much earlier against Charley.

Pinter then creates several scenes of a forlorn Emily inside the house looking out, as if now she were trapped within her own seemingly loveless denial not only of Charley, but of Jack and even Tom. Then, instead of the housekeeper who is in reality coming down the corridor, she sees Charley standing there. In another scene, Emily visits Miss Scott to reclaim the silver thimble that belonged to Jack and a little black chair with white roses painted on it, the chair associated both with Jack and, through the white roses which she has not allowed in the house, with Charlie. Pinter thus prepares us for the conclusion by showing Emily admitting into her consciousness these elements of her past.

Following two scenes that emphasize her silence and distance from Tom, Emily tells Peggy of a knot inside her, "which I have never been able to untie. It is tied so tight. I cannot untie it." The screenplay, as the tale, then concludes with Emily's declaration to Tom, set against a background of nature as the couple walk from shade into sun into shade, that Jack was her child, that she gave birth to him. Her vision of Charley kissing her breasts, making love to her, now becomes the reality that supplants the literal truth. She now sees beyond social convention and appearances to the heart of the matter:

> He [Charley] spoke out of his love, out of his great heart, out of his passion. He wanted to give me all the life of his soul and his blood. He offered it to me and I took it. I took it. I received it. I opened my life to his life. I gave myself to him.

The rigid Emily who had condemned others so readily now sees in the world not judgment but grace, a grace in the world that she has now found. "Do you understand," she asks Tom, and he affirms that he does.

Except for a few details, the conclusion is taken directly from Dinesen. In the tale, however, the conclusion represents the triumph of the artistic vision which sees more than fact. The test of "truth" lies not in a formulistic compliance of word and actuality. For the artist, the word possesses the biblical sense of being life-giving rather than stagnant, that which is loving, creative, and generative, which makes reality rather than being its slave.

Without denying this level of meaning, however, in the screenplay Pinter expands it while at the same time reducing its sentimentality. In a very real social sense which Pinter details through the additions, Jack is Emily's child in a less affirming way. The boy who died without knowing where he belonged is the offspring of her repressions and schizophrenia as well as that of her society. There remain at the end of Pinter's screenplay the dismissed servant, the harsh judgments, the cruelty which masquerades as religious righteousness, the assumptions of class superiority, the grim divide between rich and poor, slum and mansion. So, if Jack is now the child of Emily's newfound, less repressed vision of love, he is also the child of another woman's despair, shame, and death.

Though the force of the ending seems conclusive in the tale, Pinter's cinematic technique of cutting from one world to another makes a viewer less likely to see the ending as conclusive. The divides evident in his own *Party Time* remain, as does also the artistic possibility of his more recent play *Ashes to Ashes*. Emily, like Rebecca in *Ashes to Ashes*, has begun to make connections—between her past and her present, herself and "other." In a sense, like Rebecca, she has "become" that dying impoverished woman. If art has some power to create such identification and empathy—and in our time no artist can as confidently affirm that power as Dinesen did in hers—still, how far might empathy reach? In deconstructing some of Dinesen's optimism and expanding the social implications, Pinter has given us a tale for our time as well as Dinesen's.

NOTE

1. All references to the screenplay are to the unpublished manuscript. I wish to thank Harold Pinter for allowing me to read and cite from the manuscript. In the screenplay Pinter modernizes the names: Jens to Jack, Emilie to Emily, Jakob to Tom, Madame Mahler to Mrs. Jones, and Mamzell Ane to Miss Scott.

APPENDIX I

⊞

Chronology of Pinter's Film and Television Writing

1960 *The Birthday Party* televised (Associated Rediffusion Television, March 22)

A Night Out televised (BBC Third Programme, March; ABC Armchair Theatre, April 24)

Night School televised (Associated Rediffusion Television, July 21)

1961 *The Collection* televised (Associated Rediffusion Television, May 11)

1963 *The Lover* televised (Associated Rediffusion Television, March 28)

The Servant

Film version of *The Caretaker* (*The Guest*)

1964 *The Pumpkin Eater*

1965 *Tea Party* televised (BBC-1, March 25)

1966 *The Quiller Memorandum*

1967 *The Basement* televised (BBC-TV, February 28)

Accident

1968 Film version of *The Birthday Party*

1969 Film version of *The Homecoming*

The Go-Between

1972   *The Proust Screenplay* written (published 1977)

1973   *Monologue* televised (BBC-TV, April 10)

1974   *Butley*

1976   *The Last Tycoon*

1978   *Langrishe,* Go Down televised (BBC-2 Television, September 20)

1981   *The French Lieutenant's Woman*

1982   Film version of *Betrayal*

       Victory written (published 1990)

       The Hothouse televised (BBC-TV)

1985   *One for the Road* televised (BBC-TV, July 25)

       The Dumb Waiter televised

1986   *Turtle Diary*

1987   *The Dumb Waiter* televised (ABC Television, May 12)

       The Room televised (ABC Television, December 26)

1989   *The Birthday Party* televised (BBC-2, June 1)

       Heat of the Day televised (BBC)

       Reunion

1990   *The Handmaid's Tale*

       The Comfort of Strangers

1991   *The Remains of the Day* (script written, but Pinter removed his
       name from it)

       Old Times televised (BBC-TV, London)

1992   *Party Time* televised (Channel 4, London, November 17)

1993   *The Trial*

1994   *Lolita* (script written)

       The Heat of the Day televised (in America on PBS's *Masterpiece
       Theatre* (WGBH, Boston, September 30)

1996 Film version of *Landscape*

Pinter is reported to be working on an adaptation of *The Diaries of Etty Hillesum*

1997 Adaptation of *The Dreaming Child* completed

2000 Adaptation of *The Tragedy of King Lear* completed

APPENDIX II

⊞

Awards for Screenwriting

Accident: Cannes Film Festival Special Jury Prize; National Board of Review Award, one of ten best films of the year

Betrayal: Nominated for Academy of Motion Picture Arts and Sciences Awards (Best Picture, Best Screenplay Based on Material from Another Medium)

The Caretaker: Berlin Festival Silver Bear; Edinburgh Festival Certificate of Merit

The French Lieutenant's Woman: Nominated for Academy of Motion Picture Arts and Sciences Awards (Best Picture, Best Screenplay Based on Material from Another Medium); nominated for a Golden Globe (Best Screenplay—Motion Picture)

The Go-Between: British Film Academy Award (Best Screenplay); Cannes Palme d'Or award

The Last Tycoon: National Board of Review Best English-Language Film Award; Ennio Flaiano Award for Screenwriting; Donatello Prize (Italy)

The Lover: Guild of British Television Producers and Directors Award; Prix Italia (Naples) for Television Drama

The Pumpkin Eater: British Film Academy Award for Best Screenplay

The Servant: British Screenwriters Guild Award; Los Angeles Film Critics Award; New York Film Critics Best Writing Award; *New York Times* listing as one of the ten best films of the year.

SELECTED BIBLIOGRAPHY

⊞

SCREENPLAYS AND SOURCES FOR THE SCREENPLAYS

Adams, Michael. "Gatsby, Tycoon, Islands, and the Film Critics." In *Fitzgerald/Hemingway Annual: 1978*. Matthew J. Bruccoli and Richard Laymen, eds. Detroit: Gale Research, 1979, pp. 297–306.

Albee, Edward. *Lolita*. New York: Dramatists Play Service, 1984.

Anderson, William. *The Green Man*. London and San Francisco: HarperCollins, 1990.

Anonymous. "Be a Man, Mrs. Evans." *Times Literary Supplement*, October 5, 1962, p. 773.

———. "The E-Mail." "Harold Pinter Re-writing Dearden's Script for Carolco." *Hollywood Reporter*, June 10, 1994, n.p. (clipping file, Margaret Herrick Library, Academy of Motion Picture Arts and Sciences, Los Angeles).

———. "From Page to Screen." *Times Literary Supplement*, June 18, 1971, p. 695.

———. "Harold Pinter, Director." *Cinebill*, I, 7 (1974): 7 (American Film Theatre Program for *Butley*).

———. "Script Near Completion, 'Lolita' on Fast Track Toward Production." *L.A. Life*, June 26, 1995, p. 2.

Ash, John. "Contraria: Stick It Up Howard's End." *Gentlemen's Quarterly*, August 1994, p. 43.

Atkins, Irene Kahn. "Hollywood Revisited: A Sad Homecoming." *Literature/Film Quarterly*, 5 (1977): 105–11.

165

Atwood, Margaret. *The Handmaid's Tale.* Boston: Houghton Mifflin, 1986.

Baker, William and Stephen Tabachnick. *Harold Pinter.* Edinburgh: Oliver and Boyd, 1973.

Bensky, Lawrence M. "Harold Pinter: An Interview." *Paris Review,* X, 39 (1966): 96.

Betts, Ernest. "Angled for the Ladies." *People,* July 19, 1964, p. 7.

Billington, Michael. *The Life and Work of Harold Pinter.* London: Faber and Faber, 1996.

Bloom, Harold, ed. *Lolita: Modern Critical Interpretations.* New York: Chelsea House, 1987.

Bok, Sissela. *Secrets.* New York: Pantheon, 1982.

Bowen, Elizabeth. *The Heat of the Day.* London: 1948; rpt. New York: Alfred A. Knopf, 1949.

Brennan, Judy. "Not Your Average Nymphet." *Los Angeles Times,* July 14, 1995, pp. F1, F14.

Brown, Georgia. "The Servant." *The Village Voice,* November 9, 1993, p. 60.

Burkman, Katherine H. "Harold Pinter's Death in Venice: *The Comfort of Strangers.*" In *The Pinter Review: Annual Essays 1992–93.* Francis Gillen and Steven H. Gale, eds. Tampa: University of Tampa Press, 1993, pp. 38–45.

———. *The Arrival of Godot: Ritual Patterns in Modern Drama.* Rutherford, N.J.: Fairleigh Dickinson University Press, 1986.

Busch, Anita M. "'Spider man,' 'Rambo 4' in PPV pipeline." *Hollywood Reporter,* April 26, 1993, n.p. (clipping file, Margaret Herrick Library, Academy of Motion Picture Arts and Sciences, Los Angeles).

Callahan, John F. "The Unfinished Business of *The Last Tycoon.*" *Literature/Film Quarterly,* 6 (summer 1978): 204–13.

Caute, David. *Joseph Losey: A Revenge on Life.* New York: Oxford University Press, 1994.

Chopin, Kate. *The Awakening.* Chicago: H. S. Stone and Co., 1899.

Ciment, Michel. *Conversations with Losey.* London and New York: Methuen, 1985.

———. *"Accident."* In *The International Dictionary of Films and Filmakers,* vol. 1, 2nd ed. Nick Thomas, ed. Chicago: St. James Press, 1990.

Coleman, John. "Pumpkin Pie," *New Statesman*, July 17, 1964, p. 97.

Connolly, Jeanne. "*The Trial.*" In *The Pinter Review: Annual Essays 1994*. Francis Gillen and Steven H. Gale, eds. Tampa: University of Tampa Press, 1994, pp. 84–88.

Conrad, Joseph. *Victory*. London: Collins ELT, 1982; rpt. New York: Doubleday, 1957; rpt. New York: Modern Library, n.d.

Corliss, Richard. *Lolita*. London: British Film Institute, 1994.

Dearden, James. "Lolita." Unpublished screenplay. Christopher C. Hudgins's collection. (The script is labeled "Third Draft," and dated October 21, 1991, 139 mspp.)

Esslin, Martin. *The Peopled Wound: The Work of Harold Pinter*. New York: Doubleday, 1970; rpt. London: Methuen, 1992, 5th ed.

———. *Pinter: A Study of His Plays*. London: Eyre Methuen, 1973. (Originally published as *The Peopled Wound* [London: Methuen, 1970].)

Farrell, Pia. "Chargeurs gets *Lolita* Rights." *Hollywood Reporter*, December 5, 1994, p. 20.

Fitzgerald, F. Scott. *The Last Tycoon*. New York: Charles Scribner's Sons, 1941; rpt. 1969; rpt. New York: Scribner's, 1941; rpt. Scribner Classic/Collier Edition, 1986 (includes foreword by Edmund Wilson, pp. ix–x).

Fleming, Michael. "Carolco's Fire Sale." *Variety*, October 27, 1994, pp. 1, 35.

Foucault, Michel. *The Archaelogy of Knowledge and The Discourse on Language*. New York: Pantheon Books, 1972.

Fowles, John. *The French Lieutenant's Woman*. Boston: Little, Brown, 1969.

———. "Foreword." In *The French Lieutenant's Woman: A Screenplay*, by Harold Pinter. Boston: Little, Brown, 1981, pp. vii–xv.

Franklin, Olga. "Penelope Mortimer on the Problem of Marriage." *Daily Telegraph*, September 3, 1971, p. 11.

Frazer, Sir James George. *The Golden Bough*. Abr. ed. in 1 vol. New York: Macmillan, 1951.

Gale, Steven. "Art Objects as Metaphors in the Filmscripts of Harold Pinter." In *Pinter at Sixty*. Katherine H. Burkman, ed. Bloomington: Indiana University Press, 1993, pp. 163–72.

———. "*Butley* (Gray)." In *The International Dictionary of the Theatre: Volume 1, Plays*. Mark Hawkins-Dady, ed. London: St. James Press, 1992, pp. 95–96.

————. *Butter's Going Up: A Critical Analysis of Harold Pinter's Work.* Durham, NC: Duke University Press, 1977.

————. *Critical Essays on Harold Pinter.* Madison, NJ: Fairleigh Dickinson University Press, 1986.

————. "Film and Drama: The Opening Sequence of the Filmed Version of Harold Pinter's *The Caretaker* (*The Guest*)." In *Harold Pinter: A Casebook.* Lois Gordon, ed. New York: Garland, 1991, pp. 119–28.

————. *Harold Pinter: An Annotated Bibliography.* Boston: G. K. Hall, 1978.

————. *Harold Pinter: Critical Approaches.* Madison, NJ: Fairleigh Dickinson University Press, 1986.

————. "Harold Pinter." In *British Playwrights 1956 to 1995.* William Demastes, ed. Westport, CN: Greenwood, 1995, pp. 301–25.

————. "Harold Pinter." In *Encyclopedia of British Humorists.* Steven H. Gale, ed. New York: Garland, 1996, pp. 684–90.

————. "Harold Pinter's Film Version of *The Servant*: Adapting Robin Maugham's Novel for the Screen." *The Pinter Review: Annual Essays 1990.* Francis Gillen and Steven H. Gale, eds. Tampa: University of Tampa, 1990, pp. 4–20.

————. "Harold Pinter's Screenwriting: The Creative/Collaborative Process." *The Pinter Review: Collected Essays 2000.* Francis Gillen and Steven H. Gale, eds. Tampa: University of Tampa Press, 2000.

————. "'Opening Out': Harold Pinter's *The Caretaker* from Stage to Screen." *Cycnos*, XIV, 1 (1997): [113]–24

————. "The Pinter Archive II: Description of the Filmscript Holdings in the Archive at the British Library." Coauthored with Christopher C. Hudgins. In *The Pinter Review: Annual Essays 1995–1996.* Steven H. Gale and Francis Gillen, eds. Tampa: University of Tampa, 1996, pp. 101–42.

————. "The Use of a Cinematic Device in Harold Pinter's *Old Times.*" *Notes on Contemporary Literature*, X, 1 (January, 1980): 11.

Gill, Brendan. "Drawbacks of Domesticity." *New Yorker*, November 14, 1964, p. 148.

Gray, Simon. *Butley.* London: Methuen, 1971; rpt. New York: Viking, 1974.

Gussow, Mel. *Conversations with Pinter.* London: Nick Hern Books, 1994.

Hall, Adam. *The Berlin Memorandum.* London: Collins, 1965; rpt. as *The Quiller Memorandum*, New York: Simon and Schuster, 1965; paperback ed., New York: Pyramid Books, 1966.

Hall, Ann C. "Voices in the Dark: The Disembodied Voice in Harold Pinter's *Mountain Language*." In *The Pinter Review: Annual Essays, 1991*. Francis Gillen and Steven H. Gale, eds. Tampa: University of Tampa Press, 1992, pp. 17–22.

Hannah, Donald. *Isak Dinesen and Karen Blixen: The Mask and the Reality*. New York: Random House, 1971.

Hartley, L. P. *The Go-Between*. London: Hamish and Hamilton, 1953.

Higans, Aidan. *Langrishe, Go Down*. London: John Calder, 1966.

Hinchliffe, Arnold P. *Harold Pinter*. New York: Twayne, 1967, pp. 134–35

Hirsch, Foster. "*The Go-Between*." In *Critical Essays on Harold Pinter*. Steven H. Gale, ed. Boston: G. K. Hall, 1990, pp. 183–90.

———. *Joseph Losey*. Boston: Twayne, 1980.

Hoban, Russell. *Turtle Diary*. New York: Random, 1976; rpt. New York: Washington Square Press/Pocket Books, 1986.

Houston, Beverle, and Marsha Kinder. "The Losey-Pinter Collaboration." In *Critical Essays on Harold Pinter*. Steven H. Gale, ed. Boston: G. K. Hall, 1990, pp. 191–209.

Hudgins, Christopher C. "Harold Pinter's *The Comfort of Strangers*: Fathers and Sons and Other Victims." In *The Pinter Review: Annual Essays, 1995–1996*. Francis X. Gillen and Steven H. Gale, eds. Tampa: University of Tampa Press, 1997, pp. 54–72.

Irigaray, Luce. *The Sex Which Is Not One*. Trans. Catherine Porter. Ithaca, NY: Cornell University, 1985.

Ishiguro, Kazuo. *The Remains of the Day*. London: Faber and Faber, 1989; rpt. New York: Vintage, 1990.

Jones, Edward T. "Re-viewing Losey-Pinter. In *Re-viewing British Cinema, 1900– 1992: Essays and Interviews*. Wheeler Winston Dixon, ed. Albany: State University of New York Press, 1994, pp. 211–20.

Kafka, Franz. *The Trial*. 1937; rpt. New York: Alfred A. Knopf, 1937.

Kauffmann, Stanley. "Early Winter Roundup." *New Republic*, December 19, 1964, p. 29.

———. "An Elegy." *The New Republic*, December 6, 1993, pp. 32–33.

Klein, Joanne. *Making Pictures: The Pinter Screenplays*. Columbus: Ohio State University Press, 1985.

Knowles, Ronald. *Understanding Harold Pinter*. Columbia: University of South Carolina Press, 1995.

Kubrick, Stanley. *Lolita*. Film, screenplay by Vladimir Nabokov, 1962.

Kuzmanovich, Zoran. "'Sitting with the Ghost of Somebody I Had Just Killed': Humbert's Darkening Bliss." Paper presented at the Nabokov Society Meeting, Modern Language Association Convention, San Diego, December 1994.

Leahy, James. *The Cinema of Joseph Losey*. London: Zwemmer, 1967.

Losey, Joseph. "*The Servant*: Notes on the Film," p. 1. (A two-page, duplicated manuscript distributed at the premiere of the film on November 14, 1963, at the Warner Cinema in Leicester Square by Associated British–Pathé Ltd.)

McEwan, Ian. *The Comfort of Strangers*. London: Jonathan Cape, 1981, and New York: Simon and Schuster, 1981; rpt. New York: Penguin, 1989; rpt. New York: Vintage, 1994.

Mamet, David. "Lolita." Unpublished screenplay. Christopher C. Hudgins's collection. (The script is dated March 10, 1995, 138 mspp.)

Marranca, Bonnie. *Ecologies of Theater*. Baltimore: The John Hopkins University Press, 1996.

Maugham, Robin. *The Servant*. London: Falcon 1948; New York: Harcourt, Brace, 1949.

Meeker, Joseph W. *The Comedy of Survival*. New York: Charles Scribner's Sons, 1974.

Michaels, I. Lloyd. "Auteurism, Creativity, and Entropy in *The Last Tycoon*," *Literature/Film Quarterly*, 10 (1982): 110–18.

Milne, Tom. *Losey on Losey*. Garden City, NY: Doubleday, 1968.

Mitchell, Sean, and John M. Wilson. "A Lolita for the 90's." *Los Angeles Times*, June 10, 1990, "Calendar," p. 24.

Mortimer, Penelope. *The Pumpkin Eater*. London: Hutchison, 1962, and New York: McGraw-Hill, 1962, pp. 55–57.

Mosley, Nicolas. *Accident*. London: Hodder and Stoughton, 1965; rpt. Elmwood Park, IL: Dalkey Archive Press, 1985.

Mulvey, Laura. "Visual Pleasure and Narrative Cinema." In *Visual and Other Pleasures*. Bloomington: Indiana University Press, 1989, pp. 14–26.

Nabokov, Vladimir. *Lolita*. New York: Berkley, 1982; rpt. New York: Random House, 1955; rpt. New York: Vintage, 1989.

Newbolt, Sir Henry. "Anyone for. . .Tennis? Golf? Soccer? Rugby? Cricket?" In *Sports in the Movies*. Ronald Bergan, ed. London and New York: Proteus Books, 1982, pp. 112–27.

Noyes, Virginia. "Complex Compelling Chronicle of Human Foibles." *Chicago Tribune Magazine of Books*, April 21, 1963, p. 3.

Osborn, Jack R. *Croquet the Sport*. Palm Beach Gardens, FL: Farsight Communications, 1989.

Pinter, Harold. *Accident*. In *Five Screenplays*, by Harold Pinter. London: Methuen, 1971.

———. *Betrayal*. London: Methuen, 1978; New York: Grove, 1979.

———. "Between the Lines." *Sunday Times Magazine*, March 4, 1962, p. 25.

———. *The Birthday Party*. London: Methuen, 1960; rpt. in *The Birthday Party and The Room: Two Plays by Harold Pinter*, New York: Grove 1961; rpt. in *Complete Works: One*, New York: Grove, 1977.

———. *The Caretaker*. London; Methuen, 1960; rpt. in *The Caretaker and The Dumb Waiter*, New York: Grove, 1960; rpt. in *Complete Works: Two*, New York: Grove, 1977.

———. *The Collection and the Lover*. London: Methuen, 1963.

———. *The Comfort of Strangers*. In *The Comfort of Strangers and Other Screenplays*, by Harold Pinter. London: Faber and Faber, 1990, pp. 1–52. (Includes *The Comfort of Strangers, Reunion, Turtle Diary,* and *Victory*.)

———. *The Compartment*. New York: Grove, 1963.

———. *Complete Works: One*. New York: Grove, 1977.

———. *The Dreaming Child*. Unpublished screenplay. Francis X. Gillen collection.

———. *The Dumb Waiter*. London: Methuen, 1962; in *The Caretaker and The Dumb Waiter*, New York: Grove, 1961.

———. "The Examination." In *The Collection and The Lover*, by Harold Pinter. London: Methuen, 1970.

———. *Five Screenplays*. London: Methuen, 1971; rpt. New York: Grove, 1973. (Includes *The Servant, The Pumpkin Eater, The Quiller Memorandum, Accident,* and *The Go-Between*.)

———. *The French Lieutenant's Woman: A Screenplay.* Boston: Little, Brown, 1981. Foreword by John Fowles.

———. *The French Lieutenant's Woman and Other Screenplays.* London: Methuen, 1982. (Includes *The French Lieutenant's Woman, The Last Tycoon,* and *Langrishe, Go Down.*)

———. *The Go-Between:* In Pinter, *Five Screen Plays.* London: Metheun, 1971.

———. *The Heat of the Day.* London and Boston: Faber, 1989.

———. *The Homecoming.* London: Methuen, 1965; New York: Grove, 1966.

———. Interview with Christopher C. Hudgins, May 15, 1984.

———. Interview with Christopher C. Hudgins and Steven H. Gale, October 26, 1994.

———. *Landscape and Silence.* New York: Grove, 1970.

———. *Langrishe, Go Down.* In Pinter, *The French Lieutenant's Woman and Other Screenplays.* London and Boston: Faber and Faber, 1991.

———. *The Last Tycoon.* In *Harold Pinter: The French Lieutenant's Woman and Other Screenplays.* London and Boston: Faber and Faber, 1991.

———. Letter to Christopher C. Hudgins, November 11, 1994.

———. Letter to Christopher C. Hudgins, January 23, 1995.

———. Letter to Christopher C. Hudgins, March 13, 1995.

———. Letter to Christopher C. Hudgins, November 21, 1995.

———. "Lolita." Unpublished screenplay. Christopher C. Hudgins collection. (The script carries the date September 26, 1994, 188 ms. pp.)

———. *The Lover.* In *The Collection and The Lover,* by Harold Pinter. London: Methuen, 1963; rev. 1964; in *The Lover and Other Plays.* New York: Grove, 1967.

———. *Mountain Language.* London: Faber and Faber, 1988; New York: Grove, 1989.

———. *A Night Out.* In *A Slight Ache and Other Plays.* London: Methuen, 1961; rev. 1970.

———. *No Man's Land.* London: Eyre Methuen, 1975.

———. *Old Times.* London: Methuen, 1971, and New York: Grove, 1971.

———. *Party Time: A Screenplay.* London and Boston: Faber and Faber, 1991.

———. *The Pumpkin Eater*. In *Five Screenplays*, by Harold Pinter. London: Methuen, 1971.

———. *The Quiller Memorandum*. In *Five Screenplays*, by Harold Pinter. London: Methuen, 1971.

———. *The Remains of the Day*. Unpublished screenplay, 1991. Steven H. Gale collection.

———. *Reunion*. In *The Comfort of Strangers and Other Screenplays*, by Harold Pinter. London: Faber and Faber, 1990, pp. 53–100.

———. *The Room and the Dumb Waiter*. London: Methuen, 1960.

———. *The Servant*. In *Five Screenplays*, by Harold Pinter. London: Methuen, 1971.

———. "Speech: Hamburg 1970." *Theatre Quarterly*, I, 3 (1971): 3.

———. *The Trial*. Xerox copy of typescript, n.d., Steven H. Gale collection.

———. *The Trial: Adapted from the Novel by Franz Kafka*. London and Boston: Faber and Faber, 1991.

———. *Turtle Diary*. Xerox copy of typescript, n.d., Steven H. Gale collection.

———. *Turtle Diary*. In *The Comfort of Strangers and Other Screenplays*, by Harold Pinter. London: Faber and Faber, 1990, pp. 100–63.

———. *Victory*. Xerox copy of typescript, n.d., Steven H. Gale collection.

———. *Victory*. In *The Comfort of Strangers and Other Screenplays*, by Harold Pinter. London: Faber and Faber, 1990. pp. 165–226.

Proffer, Carl R. *Keys to Lolita*. Bloomington: Indiana University Press, 1968.

Pugh, Marshall. "Trying to Pin Down Pinter." *Daily Mail*, March 7, 1964, p. 8.

Rafferty, Terrence. "The Comfort of Strangers." *The New Yorker*, April 2, 1991, p. 82.

Rampton, David. *"Lolita."* In *Lolita: Modern Critical Interpretations*. Harold Bloom, ed. New York: Chelsea House, 1987, pp. 99–117. Rpt. *Vladimir Nabokov: A Critical Study of the Novels*. London: Cambridge University Press, 1984.

Rapf, Joanna E. *"The Last Tycoon:* A Nickel for the Movies." *Literature/Film Quarterly*, XVI (1988): 76–81.

Salem, Daniel. "Les Adaptations cinématographiques de Pinter," *Etudes Anglaises*, XXV, 4 (1966): 500.

Schiff, Stephen. "Lolita." Unpublished screenplay. Christopher C. Hudgins's collection. (The script carries the notations "SECOND REVISED DRAFT" and "8/22/95 Rev. Blue." The date at the lower right is July 6, 1995, 136 mspp.)

Schrader, Paul. *The Comfort of Strangers*. Film. 1990.

Sessions George, ed. *Deep Ecology for the Twenty-first Century*. Boston and London: Shambola, 1995.

Sherwood, John. "Interview with Harold Pinter." BBC European Service, in the series "The Rising Generation," March 3, 1960 (duplicated manuscript quoted in Esslin, *The Peopled Wound*, 1982, p. 36), p. 28.

Showalter, Elaine. *A Literature of Their Own: British Women Novelists From Brontë to Lessing*. Princeton, NJ: Princeton University Press, 1977.

Taylor, John Russell. *Harold Pinter*. London: Longmans, 1969, p. 20.

Trilling, Lionel. "The Last Lover: Vladimir Nabokov's *Lolita*." In *Lolita: Modern Critical Interpretations*. Harold Bloom, ed. New York: Chelsea House, 1987, pp. 5–11. Rpt. from *Speaking of Literature and Society*. New York: Harcourt Brace Jovanovich, 1980.

Tucker, Stephanie. "Cold Comfort: Harold Pinter's *The Comfort of Strangers*." In *The Pinter Review: Annual Essays, 1992–1993*. Francis Gillen and Steven H. Gale, eds. Tampa: University of Tampa Press, 1993, pp. 46–53.

Turner, Victor. *From Ritual to Theatre*. New York: PAJ Publications, 1982.

Uhlman, Fred. *Reunion*. London: Adam Books, 1971; rpt. London: Fontana, 1985; London: Penguin, 1978.

Van Gelder, Lawrence. "Lolita." *The New York Times*, April 19, 1991, p. C 10.

Wilmington, Michael. "A Pinteresque *Comfort of Strangers*." *The Los Angeles Times*, March 29, 1991, F13.

Wilson, Edmund. Foreword to *The Last Tycoon*, by F. Scott Fitzgerald. New York: Scribner Classic/Collier Edition, 1986, pp. ix–x.

Woolf, Virginia. *Mrs. Dalloway*. New York: Harcourt, Brace, and Company, 1925.

———. *A Room of One's Own*. New York: Harcourt, 1929.

———. *To The Lighthouse*. New York: Harcourt, Brace, 1927.

CONTRIBUTORS

⊞

Marya Bednerik is professor of Theatre at Kent State University where she teaches film and drama and has published in both of these areas.

Katherine H. Burkman, Emeritus Professor of English at Ohio State University, has published widely in modern drama, specializing in Harold Pinter (*Arizona Quarterly, The Pinter Review, Theatre Journal*, and elsewhere). She is on the editorial board of *The Pinter Review*, and her most recent book is a collection edited with Judith Roof, *Staging the Rage: The Web of Misogyny in Modern Drama*. The artistic coordinator of a Columbus, Ohio, writing/performing group WOMEN AT PLAY, she has directed and acted for them for the last several years.

Wheeler Winston Dixon is the chair of the Film Studies Program at the University of Nebraska–Lincoln and the author of several books on film, including *It Looks At You: The Returned Gaze in Cinema* (1995), and *The Films of Jean-Luc Godard* (1997).

Steven H. Gale is the University Endowed Chair in the Humanities at Kentucky State University, founding president of the Pinter Society, founding coeditor of *The Pinter Review*, and author of four books on Pinter (*Butter's Going Up: A Critical Analysis of Harold Pinter's Work, Harold Pinter: An Annotated Bibliography, Critical Essays on Harold Pinter*, and *Harold Pinter: Critical Approaches*).

Francis X. Gillen is Distinguished Professor of Humanities at the University of Tampa, a founding coeditor of *The Pinter Review*, and the author of numerous articles about Pinter's films.

Ann C. Hall is currently serving as English Division Chair at Ohio Dominican College and is a past president of the Harold Pinter Society.

She has recently edited a collection of essays, *Delights, Desires, and Dilemmas: Essays on Women and the Media.* She is also the author of *"A Kind of Alaska": Women in the Plays of O'Neill, Pinter, and Shepard.*

William L. Horne, an associate professor in the Department of Electronic Media and Film at Towson University, has published articles on Pinter's stagecraft and is working on a monograph on Pinter's films.

Christopher C. Hudgins is a professor of English and chairperson of the English Department at the University of Nevada–Las Vegas, vice president of the Harold Pinter Society, on the editorial board of *The Pinter Review,* and the author of several articles on Pinter's screenplays. He is also working on a volume on Pinter's films.

Edward T. Jones, a professor of English at York College of Pennsylvania, has published on Pinter's films in journals such as *Film/Literature Quarterly* and in Wheeler Winston Dixon's *Re-Viewing British Cinema, 1900–1992: Essays and Interviews.*

Mijeong Kim has a doctorate in English Literature. She is a stage actress and part-time instructor at Yeungnam University in Korea, where she teaches drama and film. She has published articles, mainly on Harold Pinter, including "Androgyny in the Male Characters of Harold Pinter." She is presently working on a comparison of the plays of Arthur Miller and Harold Pinter.

Louis Marks served as a drama producer for the British Broadcasting Corporation in London for many years. He was also the producer for Pinter's version of *The Trial,* as well as many other theatrical releases.

INDEX

177